WHERE
WISDOM
IS FOUND

WHERE
WISDOM
IS FOUND

Christ in Ecclesiastes

J. V. Fesko

Reformation Heritage Books
Grand Rapids, Michigan

Where Wisdom Is Found
© 2010 by J. V. Fesko

Published by
Reformation Heritage Books
2965 Leonard St., NE
Grand Rapids, MI 49525
616-977-0889 / Fax 616-285-3246
e-mail: orders@heritagebooks.org
website: www.heritagebooks.org

Library of Congress Cataloging-in-Publication Data

Fesko, J. V., 1970–
   Where wisdom is found : Christ in Ecclesiastes / by J. V.
Fesko.
       p. cm.
   ISBN 978-1-60178-092-8 (pbk. : alk. paper) 1. Bible. O.T.
Ecclesiastes—Commentaries. 2. Jesus Christ. I. Title.
   BS1475.53.F47 2010
   223′.807—dc22
                                            2010016008

To

Robert Riley Fesko

Contents

Acknowledgements

I was concluding a sermon series in the summer of 2007 at Geneva Orthodox Presbyterian Church, in Woodstock, Georgia. I asked the elders for suggestions for what to preach next. Elder Bud Winslow suggested that I preach through Ecclesiastes. He and his wife, Cindy, were reading the book for their devotions and found it very rich. He thought the book would also be helpful to the congregation.

I began reading commentaries on Ecclesiastes because the book was sometimes quite challenging to understand. I also contacted a colleague, Bryan Estelle, an Old Testament professor at Westminster Seminary California, and asked him for resources. In the autumn I traveled to San Diego for a theology conference. While stuck in traffic with Bryan and my current pastor, Zach Keele, we began to discuss Ecclesiastes.

What could have been a long and boring ride became a most fruitful conversation. Our discussion helped me gain better understanding of Ecclesiastes and proved more valuable than all the sessions I attended at the conference. I am much indebted to Bud, Bryan, and Zach for their suggestions on Ecclesiastes. I also thank Susan Winslow, who read the manuscript that resulted from the sermon series I preached on Ecclesiastes. She made a number of helpful suggestions and corrections. I am also grateful to Joel Beeke, Jay Collier, and the staff at Reformation Heritage Books for preparing and publishing my book. A few of the resources that I found very helpful in preparing sermons on Ecclesiastes were Charles Bridges's *Ecclesiastes*, Derek Kidner's *A Time to Dance*, and Roland Murphy's *Ecclesiastes*. I could not have written this book without the assistance of those people and resources.

I dedicate this book to our son, Robert Riley Fesko, whom my wife is carrying at this time. My prayer is that our son will never know a day apart from Christ. I also pray that Robert will draw near to Christ through Word, sacrament, and prayer, and in so doing will be conformed to Christ's image through the Spirit and renewal of his mind.

Robert, my son, I pray that our heavenly Father will give you the mind of Christ, filled with a cruciform wisdom.

Escondido, California
December 2009

Introduction

In my Christian walk of thirty-plus years, I have rarely heard Christ preached from the Old Testament. I have never heard a sermon preached from Ecclesiastes or from other wisdom literature such as Job or Proverbs. Perhaps one reason why wisdom literature in the Scriptures is ignored in preaching is that it is often challenging to understand.

People look at the Law, see its imperatives, and rest easy in their understanding of it, since it seems to offer little ambiguity. But when they go to Proverbs, they find the seemingly contradictory counsel of not answering or of answering a fool according to his folly. What is a person to do— answer or not answer? The Bible is quite aware of the ambiguity of life from a human perspective, or as Ecclesiastes says, "Life under the sun." Many Christians do not want ambiguity. Yet how many Christians wander through the gray areas of life, wishing they could find clear counsel?

Another problem with understanding a book like Ecclesiastes is that many people read the statements of wisdom in Ecclesiastes as if they were ironclad promises. Yet many of the proverbs and statements in Ecclesiastes are observations, not promises. Treating an observation like a promise can lead to bad theology. For example, "Raise up a child in the way he should go and he will not depart from it" is a proverb, not a promise. Its meaning is double-edged: raise a child well, and he will likely be a good child. But the reverse is also true: raise a child poorly, and he will likely be a bad child.

How then can parents raise a child well? They should do the right things, such as training the child in the fear and admonition of the Lord and living as examples of godliness and piety. But in the end, a child will be righteous and godly only by God's grace in Christ as applied by the Holy Spirit. There are no surefire parenting formulas for spiritual success. How many parents have seemingly done everything right and constantly interceded for a child in prayer only to watch him wander off in spiritual darkness? Such circumstances call for ultimate wisdom from the mind of Christ.

Another troubling practice I have seen is the moralistic use of wisdom literature. People have cited the book of Proverbs as if it were a book of moral principles, somewhat like what is offered in Aesop's *Fables*. They make no effort to connect the Proverbs to Christ. They read passages from the wisdom portion of the Scriptures and say, "This says nothing about Christ." Can we truly say that any portion of Scripture inspired by the Spirit of Christ has nothing to do with Christ? Are we reading Scripture right when we walk away only with morals without the conviction of our need for Christ and the assuring message of His gospel? Legalism thrives on the Law but is often frustrated by wisdom; hence, many people treat wisdom as if it were law. Wisdom, rightly understood, offers another outlook on Christ. It is a necessary part of a healthy spiritual diet because it tells us that in the midst of life's ambiguities we must lean not on our understanding but upon Christ's.

What I hope to accomplish in this book is to address such shortcomings and to offer the church a window into the wonderful world of a Christ-centered understanding of the wisdom literature of the Bible, specifically the Book of Ecclesiastes. In the pages that follow, I will explain what wisdom literature is and how it finds ultimate fulfillment in Christ, who is the incarnate wisdom of God. In so doing my prayer is that more people will love the wisdom literature of the Scriptures as they read Ecclesiastes through the lens of the crucified and risen Messiah.

1
The Futility of Life

Read Ecclesiastes 1:1–11

Some books of the Bible are challenging. Paul's letter to the Romans, for example, presents difficult doctrines. If the apostle Peter could say, under the inspiration of the Holy Spirit, that he found some things in Paul's letters difficult to understand, it is quite understandable that we struggle with certain books of Scripture. Ecclesiastes is also a book filled with difficult terrain. We find ourselves like astronauts on a seemingly barren surface as we grope for traction in its words. Some concepts appear to emerge so clearly that they inspire songs such as The Byrds' 1962 hit "Turn, Turn, Turn (to Everything There is a Season)." Other passages mystify and challenge us.

If we approach Ecclesiastes with a works-based righteousness theology, this book will make absolutely no sense. A works-based righteousness offers the simple formula: obey, and you will be blessed; disobey, and you will be punished. This approach to life and salvation takes a wisdom saying, such as "Train up a child in the way he should go: and when he is old, he will not depart from it" (Prov. 22:6), and uses it like a formula. If I do "A" (train up a child in the way he should go), then "B" (when he is old, he will not depart from it) will undoubtedly be the result. Yet we know from experience that life is not so simple. The gospel of Jesus Christ is not a formula. What happens when a parent does everything right but a child goes astray?

The immediate answer from a works-based righteousness person might be, "They must be harboring secret sin of some sort." Yet that offers no room for understanding a man like Job, who was righteous but still suffered horrific losses. It also offers no explanation for Christ, who was the perfectly righteous man who suffered everything we have suffered and more.

A nineteenth-century commentator says Ecclesiastes is a germ of the gospel that flowers in the advent of Jesus. Ecclesiastes is inspired by the same God who has breathed out the rest of the Scriptures, he says. Consequently, we can only understand what this book says in light of the gospel of Christ. If this book is ultimately about wisdom, there is no mere formula for it.

The Book of Proverbs says of wisdom: "Answer not a fool according to his folly, lest thou also be like unto him. Answer a fool according to his folly, lest he be wise in his own conceit" (Prov. 26:4–5). What should we do with that seeming contradictory advice? Do we answer or not answer a fool? The solution calls for wisdom. And the Bible tells us wisdom is not simply the applied knowledge of old men who stroke their beards and puff their pipes as they ponder life's mysteries. According to the Bible, wisdom is ultimately found in Christ Himself. The apostle Paul writes in 1 Corinthians 1:22–25:

> For the Jews require a sign, and the Greeks seek after wisdom: but we preach Christ crucified, unto the Jews a stumbling-block, and unto the Greeks foolishness; but unto them which are called, both Jews and Greeks, Christ the power of God, and the wisdom of God. Because the foolishness of God is wiser than men; and the weakness of God is stronger than men.

The only way to understand the wisdom literature in Scripture, of which Ecclesiastes is a part, is to see its termination in Christ, who is wisdom incarnate. As we proceed through various portions of Ecclesiastes, let us increasingly be aware of the weight and helplessness that the author describes, then flee to Christ to find deliverance and redemption.

Before going further, we should talk about the author of Ecclesiastes. Many people have attributed the writing to King Solomon; however, the book never explicitly claims Solomon as author. A number of names have been proposed, but in the end, Ecclesiastes is like the book of Hebrews—we do not know its author. In Ecclesiastes 1:1, the author simply identifies himself as the *Preacher* and a son of King David. Since we do not know who wrote this book, we also do not know when it was written. Some think it was written in the days of Solomon, or the tenth century B.C., while others believe it was written during the exile, or the sixth century B.C. One thing is certain: it was written within the context of Israel's covenantal dealings with the Lord and during the time of the monarchy.

Futility and Vanity

Ecclesiastes opens with a statement of seeming hopelessness: "Vanity of vanities," saith the Preacher, "vanity of vanities; all is vanity" (Eccl. 1:2). The meaning of the Hebrew word for *vanity* could also be translated as *futility*. Either way, the statement seems filled with hopelessness. What would lead the Preacher to say something like this?

The Preacher gives a number of examples to make his point: "What profit hath a man of all his labour which he taketh under the sun?" (Eccl. 1:3). This observation seems obvious, yet its wisdom seems to have fallen upon deaf ears and blind eyes throughout the centuries. Think, for example, of the Great Wall of China. In the height of its grandeur, the Great Wall stretched four thousand miles; during the Ming dynasty it was guarded by a million soldiers; two to three million people died building it; and it took several centuries to build. The Wall has been hailed as one of man's greatest achievements, for supposedly it is the only man-made object that can be seen from outer space. So in what way is this labor of man reduced to futility and vanity?

Much of the Great Wall has disintegrated over time. Literally miles of the wall vanish each year. And no, the Wall cannot be seen from outer space—that is an urban legend. So the words of the Preacher aptly describe the futility of such endeavors:

> One generation passeth away, and another generation cometh: but the earth abideth for ever. The sun also ariseth, and the sun goeth down, and hasteth to his place where he arose. The wind goeth toward the south, and turneth about unto the north; it whirleth about continually, and the wind returneth again according to his circuits. All the rivers run into the sea; yet the sea is not full; unto the place from whence the rivers come, thither they return again. All things are full of labour; man cannot utter it: the eye is not satisfied with seeing, nor the ear filled with hearing.

No matter how much man toils and labors, he is never satisfied with what he has. This spirit drives the economy in our own country. People have an insatiable thirst for things such as new cars, new clothes, and new houses. They are never satisfied. We would think that man would examine what has happened over the years and learn that those who do not learn from history are doomed to repeat it. Think of some of man's greatest achievements. What has happened to the great pyramids of Egypt? Sure, they still stand, but they are crumbling. The vast majority of them has either been destroyed or buried beneath an ocean of desert sand. The pyramids were built as great tombs in which Egyptian royalty could pack possessions for their journey into the next world, but today they are colossal monuments to the futility of life. The possessions entombed within the great pyramids have been stolen, are displayed in some museum, or are buried beneath the sand. As Ecclesiastes says, "All is vanity."

In 1918, the so-called "War to end all wars," which killed nineteen million soldiers, came to an end. World War Two, which followed, destroyed forty million soldiers and fifteen million civilians. Many wars have been waged by successive generations, each thinking *this* war would secure peace once and for all. How truly the words of the Preacher echo through the tumult:

The thing that hath been, it is that which shall be; and that which is done is that which shall be done: and there is no new thing under the sun. Is there any thing whereof it may be said, See, this is new? it hath been already of old time, which was before us. There is no remembrance of former things; neither shall there be any remembrance of things that are to come with those that shall come after (Eccl. 1:9–11).

Plato, the great Greek philosopher, was right in saying: "Only the dead have seen the end of war." The Preacher likewise says, "Vanity of vanities; all is vanity" (Eccl. 1:2).

No Futility in Christ

Vanity; is this what everything in this life is reduced to? Is the purpose and end for which God created man mere vanity? The answer to these questions comes from the apostle Paul: "For the creature was made subject to vanity, not willingly, but by reason of him who hath subjected the same in hope, because the creature itself also shall be delivered from the bondage of corruption into the glorious liberty of the children of God" (Rom. 8:20–21). Paul reflects upon *vanity*, the very subject matter of the opening of Ecclesiastes.

God subjected the creation to futility or vanity because of man's sin. When man seeks significance apart from God, forsaking the true reason for his

existence, he discovers all his labors are meaningless. All his monuments melt into nothingness.
Everything he works on is given to others. The
only way to be set free from the bondage of decay
is to receive the freedom of the glory of the children of God through Christ. The wisdom of Christ,
who is God Himself and yet perfectly human,
shows us what it means to be truly human. The
author of Proverbs shows us how wisdom and
obedience go hand in hand: "The fear of the LORD
is the instruction of wisdom; and before honour
is humility" (Prov. 15:33). Christ has given us an
example to follow, and He has redeemed us.

Those who do not know Christ are consumed
by an insatiable desire and never-ending thirst,
which result in futility and vanity. But those who
look to Christ find satisfaction, rest, and satiation
in Him, for He says: "I am the bread of life: he
that cometh to me shall never hunger; and he that
believeth on me shall never thirst" (John 6:35).
For those who see no end to their labors and toil,
Christ promises rest: "Come unto me, all ye that
labour and are heavy laden, and I will give you
rest" (Matt. 11:28). Those who are joined to Christ
know their labor is not in vain.

Those who are united to Christ do not have
to earn their place in God's presence or achieve
salvation by their labor, for Christ's labor and
obedience is what secures their salvation. Those in
Christ, therefore, do not work for salvation; they

rest, looking by faith to Christ. In this, we war not against flesh and blood but against principalities, powers, and the like. And unlike the wars of man, this war has an end, not because we die, but because Christ gives us peace and life. As the author of Hebrews tells us: "Forasmuch then as the children are partakers of flesh and blood, he also himself likewise took part of the same; that through death he might destroy him that had the power of death, that is, the devil" (Heb. 2:14). Likewise the apostle Paul tells us that Christ has conquered sin and the devil, and now sits at the right hand of the Father. In the end He will destroy death (1 Cor. 15:22–28). We find peace, rest, and conclusion in Jesus Christ, the Alpha and Omega, the beginning and the end. Apart from Christ, we find only vanity and futility. Scripture tells us the number of man is 666, three times the number of the day upon which man was created. Wicked people will never know the end of their labors or the peace of entering the eternal Sabbath rest of the Lord. In Christ, the wisdom of God, we find completion, rest, meaning, and significance, for His number is 777, the number of completion.

The danger of living in this world is that, even as Christians, we can get caught up in the vanity and futility of man. We get caught up in the rise and fall of empires, revolutions, and counter-revolutions, forgetting our union with Christ and the significance that He gives to life itself. In the movie *Bridge on the River Kwai*, Colonel Nicholson was taken prisoner by the Japanese and forced to build a bridge over which the enemy could move supplies. Colonel Nicholson tells one of his subordinates: "One day the war will be over. And I hope that the people that use this bridge in years to come will remember how it was built and who built it. Not a gang of slaves, but soldiers, British soldiers, even in captivity." Nicholson became so wrapped up in the bridge-building project that he forgot he was serving the enemy. He forgot he needed to work against the Japanese, not with them.

What is the purpose of all our labor? Do we work for the glory of man and get caught up in grand but ever-failing schemes, or are we centered upon Christ and His kingdom, which will truly last forever? The kingdom of God is found in the simplicity of teaching a child about Christ. The kingdom of God is something as ordinary as placing a tithe in the offering plate so that the gospel can go forth into the world to gather in the people of God, who are the living stones of His final temple. The kingdom of God is as simple as a prayer uttered in earnest faith in Christ: "Thy kingdom come. Thy will be done in earth, as it is in heaven" (Matt. 6:10).

Conclusion

Apart from Christ, we are crushed by the words "Vanity of vanities, saith the Preacher, vanity of vanities; all is vanity" (Eccl. 1:2). Only in Christ are we freed from the bondage of vanity and futility. Only in Christ may we know peace, rest, and the end of our labors. Christ has completed all of our labors, which we are to receive by faith alone in Him. Only with a mind guided by wisdom, or knowing the mind of Christ, will we know that life is not futility or vanity.

STUDY QUESTIONS

1. In what ways is creation subject to futility or vanity? *Through sin, all of creation is under the curse. Creation strives just as man does.*

2. In whom is wisdom ultimately found? Why is that? *Jesus Christ. He is wisdom, He is God*

3. In whom is futility removed? Why? *The children of God. Because they are redeemed they have rest and peace.*

4. In what ways can we become wrapped up in the futility of man? *material desires, politics careers, financial goals, knowledge, power*

5. Why isn't the work of the kingdom subject to the futility and vanity of man? *The work of the Kingdom is eternal and belong to our Lord, who Himself set the children free from bondage*

2
The Futility of Man's Wisdom

Read Ecclesiastes 1:12–2:6

In Ecclesiastes 1:12–2:26, the Preacher goes on a quest for wisdom and once again finds only vanity. At first glance, this conclusion might seem at odds with the Bible, for how can an inspired author of Scripture say that wisdom is futile? Before answering that question, we must feel the weight of the Preacher's quest and his crushing verdict.

The Preacher lifts the veil of hopelessness, if only for a moment, to reveal a glimmer of hope that is like a morning star. Right before sunrise a bright star appears on the eastern horizon. It is not a star but the planet Venus. Nevertheless, this morning star signals the dawn of a new day that will begin when the rising sun bursts over the horizon. The morning star in this passage signals the appearance of the Son of God, Jesus, and the revelatory light that accompanies His presence. In this light, we will ultimately see that the Preacher is right in saying that the pursuit of wisdom is vanity *if* this pursuit is done apart from Christ.

Man's Wisdom Is Vanity

The Preacher begins this passage by announcing his quest for wisdom: "I the Preacher was king over Israel in Jerusalem. And I gave my heart to seek and search out by wisdom concerning all things that are done under heaven: this sore travail hath God given to the sons of man to be exercised therewith. I have seen all the works that are done under the sun; and, behold, all is vanity and vexation of spirit" (Eccl. 1:12–14). Why would the Preacher see the pursuit of wisdom as futility? Does not the Bible extol the virtue of wisdom and its pursuit?

In his pursuit of wisdom the Preacher finds that what is crooked cannot be made straight. If we walk through the woods and find a twisted stick, nothing we do can straighten it. We might whittle away at the stick, but we would have to cut away most of the twisted stick to find some part that is the least bit straight. And that would not leave much.

Two men once made a wager. One said to the other, "I can teach a cat to be as polite and helpful as a butler." The other bet he couldn't. Weeks went by and the man trained his cat until it was time to show his friend what he had accomplished. The man's cat came forward wearing a butler's coat and carrying a silver service with tea and biscuits. The cat's owner told his friend, "Pay up! I have trained my cat to be a butler." His friend smiled, then dropped a mouse on the floor. The cat immediately dropped the tray and ran after the mouse. The point is that we cannot change the nature of anything, no matter what our efforts. The crooked cannot be made straight. As the Preacher says, even wisdom cannot change things.

Verse 17 says the Preacher expanded his search to compare wisdom, madness, and folly, but even this proved vain. The Preacher writes: "For in much wisdom is much grief: and he that increaseth knowledge increaseth sorrow" (Eccl. 1:18). The Preacher says the more he looked, the more he learned, but the more he learned, the more he discovered that his quest for wisdom brought only vexation, frustration, and futility.

In verse 17 the Preacher says he pursued the pleasures of this world and compared them with wisdom. In chapter two, he writes about what he found:

> I said in mine heart, Go to now, I will prove thee with mirth, therefore enjoy pleasure: and, behold, this also is vanity. I said of laughter, *It is mad*: and of mirth, What doeth it? I sought in mine heart to give myself unto wine, yet acquainting mine heart with wisdom; and *to*

lay hold on folly, till I might see what was that good for the sons of men, which they should do under the heaven all the days of their life (Eccl. 2:1–3; emphasis mine).

The Preacher constructed great works, houses, vineyards, gardens, parks, and irrigation pools (vv. 4–5). He bought male and female slaves, herds and flocks—more than anyone else possessed in Jerusalem (v. 7), and acquired silver, gold, and the treasures of kings and provinces. He entertained himself with male and female singers, concubines, and "the delights of the sons of men" (v. 8).

This pursuit of madness and folly was initially satisfying but eventually proved not to be so. As the Preacher says:

So I was great, and increased more than all that were before me in Jerusalem: also my wisdom remained with me. And whatsoever mine eyes desired I kept not from them, I withheld not my heart from any joy; for my heart rejoiced in all my labour: and this was my portion of all my labour. Then I looked on all the works that my hands had wrought, and on the labour that I had laboured to do: and, behold, all was vanity and vexation of spirit, and there was no profit under the sun (Eccl. 2:9–11).

The pursuit of unfettered pleasure proved futile because, as the Preacher says in verse 18: "Yea, I hated all my labour which I had taken under the sun: because I should leave it unto the man that shall be after me." He ended up hating madness and folly, because in the end, all that he gained from it would be given to others. He learned what another philosopher once said, "The living benefit from the sweat of the dead."

If the Preacher found vanity in his pursuit of madness, then surely he would find the opposite in pursuing wisdom, right? The Preacher observes what seems to be obvious: "Then I saw that wisdom excelleth folly, as far as light excelleth darkness. The wise man's eyes are in his head; but the fool walketh in darkness" (Eccl. 2:13–14b). Certainly one should profit by walking in the light, right? Yet, even this hope was crushed by the Preacher's quest:

> And I myself perceived also that one event happeneth to them all. Then said I in my heart, As it happeneth to the fool, so it happeneth even to me; and why was I then more wise? Then I said in my heart, that this also is vanity. For there is no remembrance of the wise more than of the fool for ever; seeing that which now is in the days to come shall all be forgotten. And how dieth the wise man? as the fool (Eccl. 2:14c–16).

A contemporary version of the Preacher's observation is that regardless of how we live, morally or immorally, we all face death in the end. So, like his pursuit of madness and folly, his pursuit of wisdom only made the Preacher hate life (v. 17). We envision the great king slumped upon his throne, his crown askew and his hand supporting his lowered head as he gloomily reflects upon his life of wisdom ending in death.

Yet the Preacher lifts the veil of futility for a moment as he concludes his quest for wisdom and folly, saying:

> There is nothing better for a man, than that he should eat and drink, and that he should make his soul enjoy good in his labour. This also I saw, that it was from the hand of God. For who can eat, or who else can hasten hereunto, more than I? For God giveth to a man that is good in his sight wisdom, and knowledge, and joy: but to the sinner he giveth travail, to gather and to heap up, that he may give to him that is good before God. This also is vanity and vexation of spirit (Eccl. 2:24–26).

The Preacher acknowledges that we may find satisfaction and joy in something as simple as a meal if we see that the meal comes from the hand of God. That observation was previously missing in the Preacher's quest. In pursuing wisdom, for example, he did not seek the wisdom of the Lord. So his conclusion was: "For in much wisdom is much grief: and he that increaseth knowledge increaseth sorrow" (Eccl. 1:18).

What was missing was the acknowledgement of Solomon, the author of Proverbs, that "The fear of the Lord is the beginning of knowledge: but fools despise wisdom and instruction" (Prov. 1:7). Solomon also writes: "For the Lord giveth wisdom: out of his mouth cometh knowledge and under-standing" (Prov. 2:6). Note then the Preacher's observation in verse 26: "For God giveth to a man that is good in his sight wisdom, and knowledge, and joy: but to the sinner he giveth travail, to gather and to heap up, that he may give to him that is good before God. This also is vanity and vexation of spirit." Here the veil is lifted, if only for a moment, like the morning star before the dawn, so that we can see beyond the futility of life.

Glimpsing the Light of Christ

As the morning star fades into the light of the dawning sun, we see more clearly what was once hidden beneath a veil of darkness. In the fullness of the revelation of God in Christ, we see clearly what the Preacher only whispered: God does not bestow His wisdom apart from a context and per-son—it comes through Christ and covenant. The words of the apostle Paul explain: "That their hearts might be comforted, being knit together in love, and unto all riches of the full assurance of understanding, to the acknowledgement of the mystery of God, and of the Father, and of Christ; in whom are hid all the treasures of wisdom and knowledge" (Col. 2:2–3).

Christ is the wisdom of God incarnate. He

manifested this wisdom in His fear of the Lord and His humble submission to the will of His heavenly Father. Satisfaction in life cannot be found in the pursuit of folly or the pursuit of pleasure. Even the unbelieving world understands this. Think, for example, of King Midas, who wanted the ability to touch anything and turn it into gold. He asked Dionysius, the god of gaiety and wine, to grant him this power. But soon the king realized that he might starve to death because everything he touched—including food and drink—turned to gold. When he acknowledged his greed and folly, the king was freed from the "Midas touch."

Even the world sees how self-destructive the pursuit of unchecked pleasure can be. The answer to escaping the prison of futility is not merely worldly wisdom. One can live a seemingly wise life by eating right, showing kindness to others, working for the benefit of the community, acquiring a modest amount of wealth, and paying off one's debts. But in the end, what has a person accomplished when he slips beneath the realm of the living into the darkness of death? Futility.

Only through Christ can we see the world aright. Not only do we receive Christ's righteousness by faith alone, thereby securing life beyond death and escaping the coming wrath of God against ungodliness, but we also properly perceive the things of this life. In the light of Christ, the simplest things in life become blessings from the hand of God. We see this because we have the mind of Christ. As Paul tells Timothy: "Charge them that are rich in this world, that they be not high minded, nor trust in uncertain riches, but in the living God, who giveth us richly all things to enjoy" (1 Tim. 6:17).

Only through Christ can we find contentment in something as simple as eating and drinking. If we think that food is insignificant, talk to a starving man. If we think breathing is insignificant, talk to a drowning man. If we think a cup of cool water is insignificant, talk to a man who is crossing a desert. Through Christ, we perceive the blessings of redemption as wonderful and beyond compare. We see that the simplest things in life are manifestations of the providential care of our heavenly Father. From this Christ-centered view, we see as Martin Luther once said, "The empire of the whole world is but a crust to be thrown to a dog." Likewise, Charles Bridges, a nineteenth-century commentator, noted: "What were the pleasures of Solomon's earthly paradise compared with the unspeakable delight of 'eating of the tree of life, which is in the midst of the paradise of God!'" (Rev. 2:7; Bridges, *Eccl.*, 36).

Conclusion

We should pray for the Lord's help in seeing that true wisdom can only be found in Christ. The wisdom of man only leads to folly and vanity. Learn

from the Preacher who was unable to find satisfaction and peace in his own quest for wisdom
and folly. The Preacher only found contentment
and peace when he learned that true wisdom and
knowledge come from God. God gives His wisdom,
which is hidden in Christ, to those with whom He
is pleased. Only those who are united to Christ by
faith and through the power and indwelling presence of the Holy Spirit possess the mind of Christ.
Pray, therefore, that Christ will conform us to His
image by the power of the Spirit, so that we will
receive His mind and see God's blessings in the
simple things of life.

STUDY QUESTIONS

1. Why did the Preacher's pursuit of wisdom
   and folly both result in futility? *Because both were pursued outside of Christ. Both brought sorrow, all ends in death*

2. What was missing from the Preacher's
   pursuit of wisdom? *Christ*

3. Where do we find the ultimate manifesta-
   tion of wisdom? *In Christ*

4. How can true wisdom help us to see God's
   blessings even in the simple things of life? *We see His providence and care. Seeing life through the wisdom of Christ helps us to see the wonder of His love, changes our perspective, appreciate the simple thing*

3
The Tyranny of Time

Read Ecclesiastes 3:1–15

Having looked upon the pursuit of wisdom as a futile endeavor, the Preacher now asks, "What profit hath a man of all his labour which he taketh under the sun?" (Eccl. 1:3). We have seen that apart from Christ, all of man's labor is in vain and has no purpose. As Paul reminds us: "For the creature was made subject to vanity, not willingly, but by reason of him who hath subjected the same in hope, because the creature itself also shall be delivered from the bondage of corruption into the glorious liberty of the children of God" (Rom. 8:20–21). For those in Christ, the futility of life brought on by man's sin is broken. We also saw that the Preacher's quest for wisdom and folly was ultimately pointless because the wise die just like the foolish. Finally, in desperation, the Preacher realizes that

true wisdom can only be found in fearing the Lord
and recognizing that things as simple as food and
drink come from His hand. Moreover, wisdom is
not ultimately found in the world but in the hand
of God. So we see that wisdom is found in Christ,
"in whom are hid all the treasures of wisdom and
knowledge" (Col. 2:3).

In Ecclesiastes 3, the Preacher comments on
another aspect of creation: the passing of time. This
passage may be familiar to us because it was pop-
ularized in the lyrics of "Turn, Turn," by the Byrds,
in the 1960s. Often, when a portion of Scripture is
used to fabricate a different message, it is defanged
or neutered. For example, some people who quote
John 3:16, that God so loves the world, often fail
to cite the verses that follow, which say that those
who believe in Christ receive eternal life but those
who do not believe are condemned already.

It is therefore important that we explore what
the Preacher says, not only in verses 1–8, but also
in verses 9–15. The rather quaint observations of
verses 1–8 regarding a time for everything are
followed by verses that describe it more as the
tyranny of time. Tyrants are not friends. Whether
time is friend or foe depends on the relationship
one has to the One who created time.

The Tyranny of Time

When we first read Ecclesiastes 3:1–8, we find the
simple observations that any number of people

might make. There are seasons in life for all our activities. There are happy and sad times, times of rest and work, times of peace, and times of war. All a person has to do is live for a while, and he will see the truth of these observations. As children, we often know times of joy and simplicity, when our biggest concerns are when the clock will strike 3:00 p.m. to release us from school, what we will do after school, and how only three months are left until summer! But as we grow older, we begin to realize that life is not always so fun: we have our first encounter with death in the passing of a pet or a grandparent. After we graduate from college, we find that work is more demanding than school ever was. We have good times, but now we have to tackle concerns such as health insurance, 401ks, rent, utility bills, and grocery shopping. We find that for every fun thing in life, we now have three or more not-so-fun responsibilities.

Still, we would be mistaken to think that is the extent of the Preacher's observation. As we delve deeper, we begin to sense more of the tyranny of time. In the opening eight verses of chapter 3, the word *time* is repeated fourteen times. Verse 2, for example, says there is a time to be born and a time to die. We have no control over these events. Try as we might, with the latest medical technology, botox implants, plastic surgery, or cosmetics, time waits for no one. In his poem *Invictus*, William Ernest Henley writes:

Out of the night that covers me,
Black as the Pit from pole to pole,
I thank whatever gods may be
For my unconquerable soul.

In the fell clutch of circumstance
I have not winced nor cried aloud.
Under the bludgeonings of chance
My head is bloody, but unbowed.

Beyond this place of wrath and tears
Looms but the Horror of the shade,
And yet the menace of the years
Finds, and shall find, me unafraid.

It matters not how strait the gate,
How charged with punishments the scroll,
I am the master of my fate:
I am the captain of my soul.

Time ticks away, second by second, and every man, despite his claims to control his life and be master of his own destiny, will succumb to time. He is unable to stop the march of time and to prevent his own death.

When one man succumbs to the tyranny of time and dies, others mourn. Though we might have times of laughter and dancing, as we read in verse 4, we will also experience times of weeping and mourning. We are all captive to the march of time. We will have times of joy and dancing, but those times are often not because of what we do. Rather, we dance to the various tunes of life because time thrusts them upon us. We are not the masters of our fate or the captains of our souls but rather waves that are tossed about and driven by one event or another.

Why then do we plant crops and trees and flowers? It is not because we want to but rather because it is the time to plant. Try planting a tree in the dead of winter as snow covers the ground; it will not survive. We plant trees in the spring or autumn because those are the times to plant. There are times to kill, as in war, but there are also times of peace and healing. These times are thrust upon the world, for the average soldier has no control over when he goes to war and when he may be at peace.

The tyranny of time described in chapter 3 echoes the Preacher's reflections upon the futility of life in chapter 1: "What profit hath a man of all his labour which he taketh under the sun? One generation passeth away, and another generation cometh: but the earth abideth for ever.... The thing that hath been, it is that which shall be; and that which is done is that which shall be done: and there is no new thing under the sun" (Eccl. 1:3–9). If we stopped here, all we would have left is the tyranny of time in its futility and vanity. But the Preacher goes on to say: "I have seen the travail, which God hath given to the sons of men to be exercised in it. He hath made every thing beautiful in his time: also he hath set the world in their heart, so that no

man can find out the work that God maketh from
the beginning to the end" (Eccl. 3:10–11).

If verses 1–8 are a microscopic view of the
human condition, verses 10–11 are the macro-
scopic, or big picture view. Only God knows the
beginning to the end of time. If man is left to himself and his own devices in a sin-fallen world, he
stays under the tyranny of time. But from God's
perspective of seeing things from beginning to
end, a different scene unfolds. God created man
to dwell in His presence for all eternity. This, I
believe, is something that most people, whether
believer or unbeliever, would acknowledge.

In his book *Mere Christianity*, C. S. Lewis writes
about man's relationship to time, comparing it to
a fish in water. When a fish is in its natural environment, he takes no note of the water because it
is second nature to him. But when a fish is taken
from the water, he flips back and forth gasping for
the oxygen provided in water. Likewise, we hardly
give a second thought to breathing until we find
ourselves unable to breath. If we are taken out of
our natural environment, we quickly recognize
our need for it.

As a child, I sometimes watched every second of the clock tick by, but today I notice how
quickly time moves, seemingly in weeks rather
than in seconds. How many of us say, "My, the
time is moving slowly," or, "Wow, look how
quickly time has gone by!" We notice time, writes

Lewis, because we are like a fish out of water; we are not in our natural environment. God has put eternity into man's heart, and he is restless until he enters it.

Time in the Light of Christ

How does man escape the tyranny of time? How does he enter eternity? The apostle John writes: "And this is the record, that God hath given to us *eternal* life, and this life is in his Son" (1 John 5:11; emphasis mine). God has offered us redemption that overcomes the tyranny of time, and that redemption comes through Christ. Because of man's rebellion and its consequences in a sin-fallen world, he is under the dominion of Satan, sin, and death, and all of his striving is vanity. Time becomes a tyrant because sinful man fails to acknowledge the One who controls time, whose all-provident hand guides and directs all time, and who knows the beginning from the end.

Those to whom God by the power of the Holy Spirit gives the ability to believe and trust in His Son, rise above the chaotic march of time as they see that in Christ, they have a plan, purpose, and goal. Only those who are united to Christ by faith through the indwelling of the Holy Spirit can look upon time and the seasons of life and affirm with the Preacher that everything is beautiful in its time (v. 11). Or as the Preacher says: "I know that there is no good in them, but for a man to rejoice, and to do good in his life. And also that every man should eat and drink, and enjoy the good of all his labour, it is the gift of God" (Eccl. 3:12–13).

The believer in Christ sees that all of the seasons in life are God's gifts; there is a time to be born and a time to die, a time to weep and mourn, and a time to laugh and dance, a time to tear and a time to sew, a time for war and a time for peace. What is more, all of these seasons have a purpose, for as Romans 8:28 says, "We know that all things work together for good to them that love God, to them who are the called according to his purpose." Paul continues: "For whom he did foreknow, he also did predestinate to be conformed to the image of his Son, that he might be the firstborn among many brethren. Moreover whom he did predestinate, them he also called: and whom he called, them he also justified: and whom he justified, them he also glorified" (Rom. 8:29–30). So the purpose of time and all the seasons of life is our conformity to the image of Christ.

We live in a world marred by sin, brought about by our own rebellion, in which we suffer mourning, death, and war. Through Christ we are ultimately redeemed from the consequences of our rebellion and sin, but in our mourning we are comforted by the presence of God in His Holy Spirit. In our mourning and weakness, the glory of the crucified Messiah is manifest. Paul and the apostles experienced the transformation of their weakness through the gospel of Christ. Paul writes, "For though he was crucified through weakness, yet he liveth by the power of God. For we also are weak in him, but we shall live with him by the power of God toward you" (2 Cor. 13:4). In death, the consequences of our sin and rebellion are transformed as we manifest the weakness of Christ in His own death, which then gives way to life, resurrection, and glory. As Paul says, "It is sown in dishonour; it is raised in glory: it is sown in weakness; it is raised in power" (1 Cor. 15:43).

We who are united to Christ, even in the midst of war, trial, conflict, and struggle, may be assured that our heavenly Father guides and protects us through all difficulties and uses them to conform us to the image of His Son. Moreover, we have the hope that war will eventually give way not merely to a season of peace but to the peace of eternal rest. For Revelation 21:4 says, "And God shall wipe away all tears from their eyes; and there shall be no more death, neither sorrow, nor crying, neither shall there be any more pain: for the former things are passed away." These blessings, transcending the tyranny of time, are only for those who trust in Christ and who look to Him by God-given faith. Those who refuse to repent are imprisoned by the tyranny of time and the march of the seasons. They delude themselves into thinking that they control their lives. For them, time and events have no ultimate goal of blessing and rest, but are instead things that have been thrust upon them and in the end will only judge and condemn them. Rather than seeking out the eternity that God has put in their hearts, they close their hearts to it. As Paul says in Romans 1, they suppress the truth in unrighteousness.

Conclusion

Will we surrender to God's will, repent of our sin, and seek shelter in the ark of Christ? Only in Christ will we find meaning, purpose, rest, and peace. The Preacher says, "I know that, whatsoever God doeth, it shall be for ever: nothing can be put to it, nor any thing taken from it: and God doeth it, that men should fear before him" (Eccl. 3:14). What has God done? What will endure forever? To what can nothing be added or taken away? Why do people fear the Lord? The answers are that God has done His great work in Christ through the Holy Spirit. His kingdom, which transcends time, will never fade away. Nothing can be added or taken away from the eternal riches we have in Christ because they are infinite. That is why we fear the Lord.

STUDY QUESTIONS

1. In what ways is time a tyrant? *no one can escape time, it marches on until death, all we do is controlled/subject to time.*

2. Who is the only one who transcends time? Why is that so? *God / Christ. He is outside of time*

3. What is the goal of time and the events that come with it for those who are in Christ? *They look forward to the end of time when they will be w/ Christ and all things are made new.*

4. Within the tyranny of time, can man truly be captain of his soul and master of his fate? Why not? *no, because everything is under the providence of God, all must face death, we can't control the events that will happen that alter our "plans".*

4
From Dust to Dust

Read Ecclesiastes 3:16–4:3

If we limit ourselves to man's perspective, there is seemingly no escape from the tyranny of time. However, if we look at things from God's point of view, a different picture shows us that we can look at everything that happens to us, even seemingly insignificant events, as gifts from God. In the hands of God, time becomes a crucible that He uses to conform us to the image of His Son. From this perspective Paul can say that all things work together for good for those who love God and are called according to His purpose of conforming us to Christ's image.

In Ecclesiastes 3:16–4:3, the Preacher goes on to make an observation about injustice. Perhaps we have heard the saying that absolute power corrupts absolutely. This is much like the observation that the Preacher makes here. However, there is One who holds absolute power, whose power has never been corrupted. Rather than allowing His power to be corrupted, He entered the world and submitted Himself to the corruption of human power. That action had a surprising result. Let us explore the observation of the Preacher and see how God had submitted to corrupt human power and what is the end result.

Is Death Better Than Life?

The passage begins with an observation about human judgment in courts of law. The Preacher writes: "Moreover I saw under the sun the place of judgment, that wickedness was there; and the place of righteousness, that iniquity was there" (Eccl. 3:16). The Preacher goes to the place of justice, which is presumably a court of law. In ancient Israel the courts were supposed to be places of righteousness. As Exodus 23:7 says: "Keep thee far from a false matter; and the innocent and righteous slay thou not: for I will not justify the wicked." However, the Preacher did not find righteousness in Israel's courts; he only found wickedness. Justice was being perverted in the court of law.

The place where truth was supposed to prevail became the place where truth was murdered by injustice, and wickedness sat in the judge's chair. The Preacher knew that wickedness and injustice would not go unchecked. In verse 17, he says God will judge the righteous and the wicked; He will not let injustice go unchecked. Yet the Preacher is bothered, for though he knows also the coming judgment of God when all wrongs will be righted, he must now struggle with the appalling absence of justice and the presence of death.

In verse 18, the Preacher says that God is testing man to show that he is like an animal, or beast. Note what he says in verses 19–20: "For that which befalleth the sons of men befalleth beasts; even one thing befalleth them: as the one dieth, so dieth the other; yea, they have all one breath; so that a man hath no preeminence above a beast: for all is vanity. All go unto one place; all are of the dust, and all turn to dust again" (Eccl. 3:19–20). From a human perspective, there are times when we question whether there is any justice in the world. Though man has many great abilities, even the capacity for goodness and civic righteousness, in the end, his lot is the same as a brute beast: he becomes dust. The greatest minds, the wisest sages, all succumb to death and die like dogs. Man thus has no true advantage over the beasts. For this reason the Preacher says all is vanity.

In connection with the Preacher's observation regarding the absence of justice, he asks: "Who knoweth the spirit of man that goeth upward, and the spirit of the beast that goeth downward to the earth?" (Eccl. 3:21). The Preacher asks whether there is any justice in the world since the lot of the wicked and the righteous is the same— they both die and return to the dust. Who knows whether there is anything beyond the grave? Who knows whether the wicked will be punished or the righteous vindicated? The Preacher therefore says: "Wherefore I perceive that there is nothing better, than that a man should rejoice in his own works; for that is his portion: for who shall bring him to see what shall be after him?" (Eccl. 3:22). The Preacher says that in the face of what lies hidden behind the veil of death man can at least take plea- sure in his labor. In other words, man can enjoy what he does in the present.

The Preacher then expands his observation on the unjust courts to the world at large. What he sees there does not encourage him, for he sees the tears of the oppressed and the great power of the oppressors. He laments that no one is present to comfort the oppressed in their affliction (Eccl. 4:1).

This is the case throughout history. People who are oppressed by a tyrant are promised by revolutionaries that they will be freed from the oppressor. People rally behind the revolutionaries, often paying the price of their own blood, only to become oppressed by their liberators. George Orwell's *Animal Farm* tells how pigs on a farm are led by Napoleon, the head pig, to overthrow their human oppressor. The animals create a commune where everyone is considered equal and all human activities are banned. Yet slowly the pigs take up the practices of their human oppressors. They eat human food, sleep in beds, and walk on their hind legs. At one point one of the animals says to the pigs, "I thought we were supposed to be equal and share everything alike," to which the pig responds, "We are equal, it's just that some are more equal than others."

This type of injustice leads the Preacher to say: "Wherefore I praised the dead which are already dead more than the living which are yet alive. Yea, better is he than both they, which hath not yet been, who hath not seen the evil work that is done under the sun" (Eccl. 4:2–3). If life is filled with unrelenting oppression of the weak by the strong, then perhaps death is better than life. Maybe we should all return to dust. Maybe it is better not to be born than to enter a world where the powerful oppress the weak. We can say with the Preacher that in the end, there appears to be no justice in the world. Even if a person receives justice in this life, he dies just like a person who has been condemned for his crime. Both die like brute beasts, and all return to dust.

Justice in the Light of Christ

The Preacher says something in Ecclesiastes 3:17 that should give us pause: "I said in mine heart, God shall judge the righteous and the wicked: for there is a time there for every purpose and for every work." The only power that never corrupts is the power of the living God. The Scriptures clearly reveal that God is upright, and holy. He does not sin or cause sin (James 1:17). God never commits an injustice, for His power is absolutely incorruptible. The necessary implication of the Preacher's observation here is that God *will* judge the righteous and the wicked. If God will do this, we have hope for life beyond the grave.

As we read Ecclesiastes we should envision the authors of Ecclesiastes, Psalms, and Proverbs having a three-way discussion about wisdom. These books often make similar observations about wisdom. Note how the psalmist reflects upon the same themes that the Preacher considers, namely, the seeming injustice of the wicked and the righteous both returning to dust, and both dying regardless of their conduct:

> For he seeth that wise men die, likewise the fool and the brutish person perish, and leave their wealth to others. Their inward thought is, that their houses shall continue for ever, and their dwelling places to all generations; they call their lands after their own names. Nevertheless man being in honour abideth not: he is like the beasts that perish. This their way is their folly: yet their posterity approve their sayings. Like sheep they are laid in the grave; death shall feed on them; and the upright shall have dominion over them in the morning; and their beauty shall consume in

the grave from their dwelling. But God will
redeem my soul from the power of the grave:
for he shall receive me (Ps. 49:10–15).

The psalmist fleshes out what is implicit in the
Preacher's statement. From a human perspective,
it seems there is no justice, for the wicked and the
righteous perish just like brute beasts. But there is
hope, for there will be a judgment of the wicked
and an exaltation of the righteous. Let us consider
the way in which God will bring this about.

We will not simply move from life to death,
then watch with glee as the wicked get what is due
to them, for we must remember that all the injustice and oppression in this life can be traced back
to the sin of our first parents. Adam's sin is our
sin. If God were to dispense justice, all of us would
be guilty of wickedness, and all of us would suffer
under the just wrath of God, the Supreme Judge.

But we know from the New Testament that
God entered the world and submitted to corrupt
human power. God did this by sending the God-
man, Jesus, to enter the sin-fallen world so that
He might redeem His people. So God does not
simply look down upon human suffering and
observe man from His post the way the Greek
gods were said to have done, always watching
but rarely intervening. God not only intervened;
He also entered into the realm of human suffering
that man brought upon himself through his own

rebellion and sin. The God-man lived a perfect life of obedience, then submitted to a corrupt human court. As the apostle Peter writes, Christ "when he was reviled, reviled not again; when he suffered, he threatened not; but committed himself to him that judgeth righteously" (1 Pet. 2:23).

However, God does not ignore the demands of His justice and simply write off our sin, for this would defy His command to Israel that they not acquit the guilty. Rather, the God-man bore the condemnation due to His people on their behalf. In this way, as Paul writes, God is both the just and justifier (Rom. 3:26). God justifies the ungodly, but not by being unjust, for He condemned our sin in Christ. God condemned our sin in Christ but He also raised Him from the dead, reversing the unjust verdict and punishment that was brought against His Son by a corrupt court. The life, death, resurrection, and ascension of Christ give us hope in a world of injustice and oppression. When we see injustice against the people of God, we know that this wickedness will not go unchecked. When we see the people of God oppressed by the mighty, we know that Christ, the crucified God-man, has suffered on their behalf and will in the end deliver them from their suffering.

Martin Luther once wrote, "It is not sufficient for anyone, and it does him no good to recognize God in his glory and majesty, unless he recognizes him in the humility and shame of the cross" (Heidelberg Disputation, § 20). In Christ's suffering and death, we may hope that God through Christ will right all wrongs and deliver His people from the consequences of their sinful rebellion. Man's end is not like that of the brute beasts because it is invested with dignity, glory, and eternity through the resurrection of Christ. If this is so, then we who are united to Christ by faith should also be mindful of whose image we are being renewed to bear. If we are marked by the indelible pattern of the crucified Christ, we will live out the sacrificial love of Christ. We will not engage in unjust conduct but uphold truth and righteousness at all costs.

Conclusion

We may rejoice that one day God will judge the wicked and redeem the righteous. We may rejoice that God has sent His Son to stand in our place as sinners who are justly condemned but have nevertheless received the mercy and grace of God in Christ. We give thanks that God has redeemed His people by entering our suffering and by submitting to the judgment of a sin-fallen world so that we might be redeemed from it. If we desire to see the glory of God in the redemption of His people, it must also be through the shame and suffering of the cross. We should thus pray that God will reveal His righteousness and holiness to us so that as disciples of the crucified Christ we will manifest His ways to others and thereby bring them a taste

of the coming righteousness, justice, mercy, and
grace of heaven brought down to earth.

STUDY QUESTIONS

1. If we look at things from a human perspective, in what ways does it seem like
   our conduct, righteous or wicked, does
   not matter? *Because, from that perspective, everyone ends up in the same place.*

2. What statement by the Preacher tells us
   that there will be a final reckoning? *V 17. God will judge the righteous and wicked*

3. Can we stand as righteous in God's sight
   by our own good works? Why not? *no. all sin, even the Redeemed*

4. In what way has God submitted himself
   to the injustice of wicked men? *By taking on human flesh and dying for us.*

5. How does the crucified Christ shape His
   disciples in their conduct towards the
   weak and suffering people of the world? *He is our example, and we follow Him. He was kind, loving compassionate, etc. By our sufferings we become more sensitive to the needs and sufferings of others.*

5
Two are Better Than One

Read Ecclesiastes 4:4–16

In the previous chapter, the Preacher noted two apparent injustices in the world: first, that man, wicked or righteous, appears to have the same end as beasts; both return to dust. Second, the weak are oppressed, and no one seemingly takes up their cause. In all of the Preacher's observations, he reflects upon life in a sin-fallen world because of Adam's rebellion against God.

Jesus entered this sin-fallen world and delivered us from the injustices of the world by submitting to them and promising to right all wrongs, but more importantly He delivered us from the consequences of our own sin. His resurrection proves that the wicked and the righteous do not have the same end. Christ will judge the wicked and redeem the righteous who look to Him by faith alone. In this regard, the oppressed always have someone to comfort them: Jesus, who suffered and died so that we might live and who comforts us in our trials through the Holy Spirit.

The Preacher now makes further observations about life in this sin-fallen "life under the sun." He sees more examples of vanity, such as the vanity of covetousness and laziness. Between these book-ends of vanity, the Preacher makes the positive observation that a threefold cord is not quickly broken. It is important to see what the Preacher means by this observation, how it relates to Christ and the church, and how it will help us find blessing, hope, and joy.

Observations about Life

Finding True Contentment (vv. 4–7)
In Ecclesiastes 4:4–7, the Preacher implicitly acknowledges the truth of the tenth commandment, which prohibits coveting. He says, "Again, I considered all travail, and every right work, that for this a man is envied of his neighbour. This is also vanity and vexation of spirit" (Eccl. 4:4). If we expect to find happiness in accumulating as many possessions as our neighbors, we will never truly find happiness, says the Preacher. We will not find contentment, either, for how could we find satisfaction in someone else's dreams and goals? What if our neighbor is seeking contentment in keeping

up with *his* neighbors? Who, in the end, defines contentment for us? Marketing gurus tell us we will find contentment if we buy the product they sell but then drive us to further discontent when they advertise the next year's model and tell us we will not be happy unless we buy *that* new model. This is striving after the wind; it is vanity.

The flipside of the coin is also vanity, for the Preacher says, "The fool foldeth his hands together, and eateth his own flesh" (Eccl. 4:5). Aesop's fable of the grasshopper and the ant is an example of this kind of vanity. The ant dutifully worked to gather food and built his home, knowing that winter was coming. All that time, the grasshopper was relaxing and singing and enjoying the warmth of summer. When winter came, the grasshopper found himself without food and shelter. He asked the ant for help, only to be told: "Idleness brings want. To work today is to eat tomorrow. It is best to prepare for the days of necessity."

The Preacher offers us a balance between covetousness and slothfulness by saying, "Better is a handful with quietness, than both the hands full with travail and vexation of spirit" (Eccl. 4:6). It is better to live modestly than to spend all our efforts trying to keep up with our neighbors. It is not only foolish to chase the wind of envying our neighbor's possessions, but it is also idolatrous to do so, for that turns God's good gifts into idols.

Let us not forget the main thrust of the tenth commandment.

Laboring with Others (vv. 7–12)

The Preacher now builds on his observation of the pursuit of possessions driven by envy by asking, why do we labor and toil alone? For whom are we amassing wealth? This kind of labor is also vanity, the Preacher says. One way to find satisfaction in work is to do it in company with another. The Preacher advises:

> Two are better than one; because they have a good reward for their labour. For if they fall, the one will lift up his fellow: but woe to him that is alone when he falleth; for he hath not another to help him up. Again, if two lie together, then they have heat: but how can one be warm alone? And if one prevail against him, two shall withstand him; and a threefold cord is not quickly broken (Eccl. 4:9–12).

Marriage is more satisfying than living alone, for loneliness often leads to the excessive pursuit of wealth and possessions, the Preacher says. So is working with another, for companions may offer each other mutual assistance. When one falls, the other may help him up. Two can keep each other warm and help each other against outside attack. These observations are certainly true of godly marriages. They are also true of team sports.

Teams made up of individuals seeking their own glory usually fail, whereas teams of individuals working together for a common goal usually win against opponents.

Aesop's fable "The Four Oxen and the Lion" illustrates this point well. A lion often lurked in a field where four oxen grazed. Every time the lion tried to attack the oxen, they would form a circle, nose to tail, so that whenever the lion approached, he would be met by menacing horns. The oxen, however, began bickering among themselves and eventually separated, each to its own corner of the field. The lion then attacked each of the oxen separately, making a meal of each. The truth is simple: divided we fall, united we stand. A threefold cord is not easily broken.

Uniting for the Wrong Purpose (vv. 13–16)
We might think, "Aha! Since a threefold cord is not quickly broken, all people have to do is unite around a common cause rather than working as individuals, and they can accomplish anything they set their collective mind to do." Not so fast, says the Preacher. In the closing verses of chapter 4, the Preacher observes how people may become united in discontentment.

For example, people may become disenchanted with an old and foolish king because he no longer takes sound counsel, the Preacher says. The old king forgets his own rise from poverty to power, then disregards the plight of his people. The people feel betrayed, so they remove the king and replace him with a poor but wise youth. The new king assumes his place, only to disappoint his people in another way. So the Preacher observes: "There is no end of all the people, even of all that have been before them: they also that come after shall not rejoice in him. Surely this also is vanity and vexation of spirit" (Eccl. 4:16). The people become disenchanted with their new king and look for ways to replace him. This too is vanity, a striving after the wind, says the Preacher.

Union with Christ

Given these observations, should we think that two are better than one is discounted by the discontentment of a united people? Not at all. If we limit ourselves to human observation alone, then, yes, we are left with vanity. But what is impossible with man is possible with God. The Preacher's observations on the blessings of marriage are ultimately realized in Christ's marriage to His bride, the church. Christ redeems us from the solitary and idolatrous pursuit of contentment that puts us on the throne of our lives and seeks to gratify our insatiable lust for things. We make ourselves the center of our universe only to discover that everything we thought would satisfy us leaves us empty. Even worse, we are liable to God's just condemnation for our failure to worship Him, and Him alone.

Christ delivers us from our idolatrous quest for self by showing us that what is His becomes ours (righteousness), and what is ours (sin) becomes His. He bears the penalty of sin due to us, and we receive His righteousness so that we can stand in God's presence. In this way, two are better than one as we receive the good reward for our bridegroom's toil. Moreover, when we fall, whether into trial or sin, Christ lifts us up, enabling us to persevere and to overcome. Christ sanctifies us and cleanses us from sin so that, as Paul writes, He may present us to the Father as a spotless bride. Christ also stands with us, defending and protecting us from our greatest enemies: Satan, sin, and death.

At the same time, we struggle with sin and tend to wander from God, forgetting our first love. The dangers of idolatry do not fade the moment we are saved. Paul describes our struggle with sin in Romans 8:12–13: "Therefore, brethren, we are debtors, not to the flesh, to live after the flesh. For if ye live after the flesh, ye shall die: but if ye through the Spirit do mortify the deeds of the body, ye shall live." In our struggle for sanctification, we must remember that two are better than one, for alone, we cannot be sanctified. Only through Christ and the Spirit can we be sanctified. I have nevertheless met professing Christians who believe they can do just fine apart from Christ, apart from the means of grace, and apart from the body of Christ, the church.

Apart from Christ and the Spirit, we will grow discontent and once again seek satisfaction in idolatry. Like the people who were discontent with the old foolish king, we will seek another leader, only to be dissatisfied with his replacement. We must remember that only by abiding in Christ will we find true contentment in life (John 15:5–8). In His statement about the vine and the branches, Christ links union with Him with fruitfulness and contentment. He says that union fuels unity in the church (John 15:11–13). As individual members of the church are drawn closer to Christ, they in turn are drawn closer to one another. Thus "two are better than one" applies not only to our union with Christ, but also to the fellowship we have within the church.

So often we think we need only Christ. In one sense this is true; Christ alone can save us from sin. However, we must never forget that we have not been saved as individuals to remain individuals but to be individuals incorporated into the church. The next time you are in church, take a look around. You may not think you need the people sitting around you, but you do! The Bible tells us that we need one another, and there are no unimportant members of the body of Christ. For if one falls, the other will lift him up. Woe to the one who is alone, for when he falls he has no one to lift him up. Do we lift up others to build them in Christ? Or are we critical and judgmental about them? The words of Christ and Ecclesiastes teach us that we must assist our brother or sister in Christ, whatever the need.

Conclusion

As we reflect upon the Preacher's words, realize that alone we fail but united we stand. Our unity must be grounded in Christ alone through His Holy Spirit. Pray that God will deliver us from our idolatrous pursuit of selfish desires, which results in eternal condemnation for the unrepentant. Pray that Christ will enable us to turn from idolatry and place all our faith in Him, preserving us as we grow in sanctification. Also, remember that we have been united to Christ *and* to His body, the church. Seek to love, assist, and share with others in the church what we have received from Christ. Two are better than one, and a threefold cord is not quickly broken.

STUDY QUESTIONS

1. Why are two better than one in the life of sanctification? *Alone we can not be Sanctified.*

2. Is it possible for people to be united for the wrong reasons? In what ways? *Yes, United by a cause that may not be good.*

3. To whom must we be united to find true contentment in life? *Jesus Christ*

4. How does our union with Christ imply unity with others in the church? *The church, made up of many members is the Bride*

5. Where else in redemption do we find the "two are better than one" principle? *Christ and the Holy Spirit*

When we are united to Christ, His righteousness becomes our; He took on our sins

6
Fear God

Read Ecclesiastes 5:1–7

So far the Preacher has largely confined his observations to the outside world. Now he turns his attention to the temple and makes some observations about the worship of God. In particular, he turns his attention to those who worship God.

The Preacher's tone is quiet here, but his words are razor-sharp. Unlike the prophets of the Old Testament who are sharply critical of those who worship God but are hypocrites, the Preacher targets people who come to the temple with good intentions but only worship half-heartedly. He especially targets those who make a commitment to the Lord, then never get around to fulfilling it. Though the Preacher's observations are from old, they are still relevant today. Let us examine what the Preacher says within the greater context of

Scripture as well as the life, death, and resurrection of Christ. In so doing, we will see that we are incapable of fearing God, but Christ has offered our heavenly Father what we are unable to give. Through the Holy Spirit, Christ enables us to fear God and to offer Him worship that is good, acceptable, and pleasing in His sight.

Observing the House of God

The Preacher opens Ecclesiastes by saying: "Keep thy foot when thou goest to the house of God, and be more ready to hear than to give the sacrifice of fools: for they consider not that they do evil" (Eccl. 5:1). This observation is echoed in other portions of Scripture, such as Proverbs 15:8: "The sacrifice of the wicked is an abomination to the LORD: but the prayer of the upright is his delight." Or Proverbs 21:3: "To do justice and judgment is more acceptable to the LORD than sacrifice." The Preacher is making a scathing denouncement of formalism in worship.

He lambasts the person who comes to the temple, making an ostentatious show of what he is doing in offering sacrifices before the Lord. The Preacher calls such people *fools*. In the Bible, *fool* is a great insult. Psalm 14:1 states that *the fool* says in his heart there is no God. By contrast, the Preacher says it is better to come to the temple to simply listen. But in listening the Preacher does not mean we should simply sit quietly. Rather, the verb *to listen* means to hear what is said, then do it. In other words, we are to obey the words said by the preacher. The prophet Samuel also makes this point when he asks King Saul, "Hath the LORD as great delight in burnt offerings and sacrifices, as in obeying the voice of the LORD? Behold, to obey is better than sacrifice, and to hearken than the fat of rams" (1 Sam. 15:22). Notice the parallelism between *to obey* and *to hearken* (or listen); they mean the same thing, for can one truly say he has heard the Lord's command if he does not obey it?

Samuel's comment was made in response to Saul's disobedience to the Lord's command to completely destroy the Amalekites. Saul disobeyed God by saving some of the Amalekites, then sacrificing some of their animals to God. Samuel's response was: "What meaneth then this bleating of the sheep in mine ears, and the lowing of the oxen which I hear?" (1 Sam. 15:14). The teaching that obedience is better than sacrifice is repeated by several Old Testament prophets: in Psalm 40:6–8, Proverbs 21:3, Isaiah 1:11–13; 16, 17, Jeremiah 7:22–23, Micah 6:6–8, and Hosea 6:6.

To illustrate his point, the Preacher says in verses 2 and 3, "Be not rash with thy mouth, and let not thine heart be hasty to utter any thing before God: for God is in heaven, and thou upon earth: therefore let thy words be few. For a dream cometh through the multitude of business; and a fool's voice is known by multitude of words." The

Preacher then expands his comments about the words of a fool. He says a fool is quick to speak and then utters many words. He likens the words of a fool to a dream, which is not real, though it often stirs much thought. Who has not been shaken in the night by a dream? But when we wake up, what we thought was so real turns out to be only a dream. So in verse 3 the Preacher says that like a dream comes with much business, so a fool sounds off with many words. One commentator says the Preacher here likens the words of the fool to "verbal doodling," which, in the end has no real effect. The words are useless and empty.

The Preacher also makes the point in verse 7: "For in the multitude of dreams and many words there are also divers vanities" (Eccl. 5:7). Rather than uttering the babblings of a fool, we are told by the Preacher:

> When thou vowest a vow unto God, defer not to pay it; for he hath no pleasure in fools: pay that which thou hast vowed. Better is it that thou shouldest not vow, than that thou shouldest vow and not pay. Suffer not thy mouth to cause thy flesh to sin; neither say thou before the angel, that it was an error: wherefore should God be angry at thy voice, and destroy the work of thine hands? (Eccl. 5:4–6).

We must do what we vow to do. Implicit in this command is that, unlike a fool who rashly utters many words, a wise person is slow to commit himself, and when he does, is a person of few words. Though a person makes fewer promises, he will undoubtedly be more trustworthy than a fool because he will be more able to fulfill the promises he makes.

Would you rather be someone who makes a hundred promises and keeps only a few of them, or a person who makes a few promises and keeps them all? The Preacher's point here is that a person might sound flowery and pious as he approaches the Lord, but his words are empty if they are only lip service. It is better to say little and to "Fear thou God."

Engaging in True Worship

The observations of the Preacher are repeated in the words of Jesus, such as: "Not every one that saith unto me, Lord, Lord, shall enter into the kingdom of heaven; but he that doeth the will of my Father which is in heaven" (Matt 7:21). Like the Preacher, Jesus strongly reprimanded people such as the scribes and Pharisees for their hypocrisy, saying: "Even so ye also outwardly appear righteous unto men, but within ye are full of hypocrisy and iniquity" (Matt. 23:28).

Christ was just in denouncing the formalism of the Pharisees. However, let us not stop here. Because of the abiding presence of sin, we are incapable of offering God the obedience that He requires. If we look intently at the Law and its demands, we see that it addresses matters of the heart in terms of deeds and motives and thoughts. We find ourselves at the foot of a great fiery mountain, whose heights we are ill-equipped to climb. The mountain we are incapable of climbing is Mt. Sinai, from which the Law was given and on which the Lord dwells, surrounded by fire and clouds of dark smoke. We are as ill-equipped to climb this mountain as we are of offering God the obedience that He requires. However, our inability does not make us eager to obey God, but rather to flee from Him in fear or rebellion.

The Israelites stood in fear at the foot of Mt. Sinai and told Moses to go to the top, while they engaged in idolatry. The apostle Paul writes about both Jew and Gentile, saying, "There is none righteous, no, not one.... There is no fear of God before their eyes" (Rom. 3:10, 18). So we find ourselves in a quandary. How can we offer God something we cannot possibly give? When Paul says no one is righteous, the only exception is Jesus Christ. The book of Hebrews gives an antiphonal response to this dilemma by pointing to Christ. Hebrews 10:7 says, "Then said I, Lo, I come to do thy will, O God." Christ obeyed every jot and tittle of the law.

Think of the extent of His obedience. Though Christ was poor, He did not envy the possessions of others. Though at times He was hungry, He did not covet food. He even denied Himself food when

He could have turned stones into bread. When He looked upon another woman, He never did so with lust in His heart, but only as a person who needed His mercy and grace. Though Christ had every opportunity to be angry or impatient with His dimwitted and quarrelsome disciples or the wicked, conniving religious leaders, He met such sinful conduct with love. Think of what the dying Christ said on the cross as He bore the ridicule of religious leaders: "Father, forgive them; for they know not what they do" (Luke 23:34).

As we contemplate the perfect obedience of Christ, we see His perfect righteousness and become more aware of our own unrighteousness. How often we have coveted the possessions of others, filled our bellies until stuffed, looked upon someone with lust in our heart, crossed the line from righteous to hate-filled anger, or returned the wrong of someone by being hateful in return. When we look to Christ by faith alone, every one of our sins is taken away. What was ours becomes Christ's, and what is Christ's becomes ours as we receive His imputed righteousness and our sin is imputed to Him. When God looks upon us, He sees not our sinfulness but the perfect righteousness of Jesus Christ. We are robed in His glorious obedience.

Hebrews says Christ offered the obedience that God required of us, but He also offered His life as the perfect sacrifice, thus removing the wrath of God from us. Christ paid the penalty on our

behalf. When Christ saves us by the effectual calling of the Word by the power of the Holy Spirit,
we are given the ability to believe in Christ and to
trust in His work, but we are also given the ability to fear the Lord. Apart from Christ, the words
of the Preacher are an insurmountable peak. They
are words that descend from the fiery top of Mt.
Sinai and only bring condemnation. But through
Christ, the words of the Preacher no longer condemn us, for they are written on our hearts
by Christ through the Spirit. The words of the
Preacher therefore become sage counsel for us.

We can now understand the Preacher's intent
in saying that to listen is better than to offer the
sacrifice of fools, and that we must come to the
gathering of God's people, not hoping that God
will be pleased with us if we just go through the
motions. Rather, we realize that He is pleased only
when we come, trusting in Christ and praying that
He will enable us to offer the sacrifice of praise out
of genuine thanks for the mercies we have received
in Christ. When we gather for worship, we will
not be rash and utter foolish promises to impress
those around us. Instead, we will come knowing
that the Lord knows the motives of the heart, and
desiring to make promises to the Lord and fellow
believers through faith in Christ. Our motive in
every vow, promise, and commitment will not be
to impress God or those around us, but to serve
the Lord and follow His calling. Our faithfulness

will be manifest in our lives. We will strive to be a people of few words, and what few words we utter will be words of praise and thanksgiving for the work of Christ and heartfelt requests that He will enable us to be faithful in upholding every promise we make, whether to God or people.

Conclusion

As the Preacher says, let us guard our steps when we come to the house of God to be with His people gathered in worship and to fear the Lord. We should not fear God in trembling and dread of punishment, for that does not characterize someone who knows Christ. Through Christ we have peace with God. Rather, we should fear God out of respect and honor, trusting God in Christ by the Holy Spirit and desiring to manifest Christ's obedience before God and the world.

STUDY QUESTIONS

1. What is formalism or hypocrisy in worship? _Outward appearances, lip-service, not obeying, many showy words_

God knows the heart.

2. Why does God despise such worship? What does He require? _Obedience, trust and faith in Christ._

3. Who is the only one who has obeyed God perfectly and has listened to the Lord? In what way has He done that? _Jesus Christ. He has 100% fulfilled and kept the Law._

4. Why is it better to utter fewer promises than many? _It is easier to keep fewer promises because you never know what may arise to keep you back from fulfilling your promise._

The verb to listen means to hear, then do. Obey God.

7
The Vanity of Wealth

Read Ecclesiastes 5:8–6:9

In the last chapter the Preacher offered reflections on the temple, worship, and a fool who speaks quickly and makes many promises, then fails to fulfill them. He likened such a person to a dream that may bother us and keep us up at night but is not real. The fool's words are like verbal doodles; they are vanity. It is better to come to the temple to listen and to obey, the Preacher says, for obedience is better than sacrifice.

Jesus has offered the obedience that the Lord requires as well as the sacrifice that cleanses us of our sins. Now the Preacher makes observations about the vanity of wealth and honor. If we pursue only the things of this world, we will eventually discover that the pursuit of wealth and honor is vanity. The Preacher offers a more positive option, which is to look for satisfaction in a simple meal. Implicit in this is the awareness of the providence of God, for every good and perfect gift comes from the hand of God. However, the only way to be able to enjoy such simple pleasure is to first find contentment in Christ.

Money and Greed

The Preacher begins with an observation that appears critical of government. In verses 8–9, he says that if a leader is oppressive, the Israelites need not worry because a local ruler is overseen by a regional ruler, and a regional ruler is overseen by a higher official. With a touch of sarcasm, the Preacher says the oppressor will not be held accountable for the sake of truth or justice but to keep things orderly for the sake of his cultivated fields (v. 9). In other words, the king is driven by greed more than justice. The Preacher then says about greed,

> He that loveth silver shall not be satisfied with silver; nor he that loveth abundance with increase: this is also vanity. When goods increase, they are increased that eat them: and what good is there to the owners thereof, saving the beholding of them with their eyes? The sleep of a labouring man is sweet, whether he eat little or much: but the abundance of the rich will not suffer him to sleep (vv. 10–12).

A greedy man is not satisfied even when his coffers are full and his belly is stuffed, for there is always something more to get. Greed is an equal opportunity sin; it is not reserved merely for the wealthy.

It is easy to see greed in the wealthy. Think, for example, of the salaries of professional athletes. Almost every year young rookie athletes are wooed by teams offering them higher salaries, signing bonuses, and other amenities, even before they have proved themselves on the field. When asked what they think of such salaries, a rookie's likely response is that he wants to be the highest paid player in his position. Likewise, the corporate world offers CEOs outrageous salaries. According to some statistics, CEO salaries for Fortune 500 companies are 500 to 1, meaning the CEO makes more by lunchtime on his first day than the average employee earns all year. Or who can forget the shoe closet of Imelda Marcos, wife of the former president of the Philippine Islands? She had 15 mink coats, 508 gowns, 888 handbags, and 1,060 pairs of shoes.

Greed knows no boundaries. It affects the wealthy and the poor. But it also affects the middle class. Greed drives people into debt so they can satisfy their lust for possessions. Yet many fail to see that what promises to satisfy them in the end never does. The Preacher writes:

> There is a sore evil which I have seen under
> the sun, namely, riches kept for the owners
> thereof to their hurt. But those riches per-
> ish by evil travail: and he begetteth a son,
> and there is nothing in his hand. As he came
> forth of his mother's womb, naked shall he
> return to go as he came, and shall take noth-
> ing of his labour, which he may carry away
> in his hand. And this also is a sore evil, that
> in all points as he came, so shall he go: and
> what profit hath he that hath laboured for
> the wind? All his days also he eateth in dark-
> ness, and he hath much sorrow and wrath
> with his sickness (Eccl. 5:13–17).

In a sin-fallen world, man works by the sweat
of his brow, but regardless of what he accumu-
lates, takes nothing with him when he dies. His
work thus is toiling after the wind. The Preacher
says that in the process of laboring to accumulate
possessions, a man worries, sweats, lies awake
at night, and works himself silly. Yet almost as
soon as he acquires wealth, he may lose it in a
bad business venture and be stricken by worries
over his lost fortune. The Preacher observes: "Yea,
though he live a thousand years twice told, yet
hath he seen no good: do not all go to one place?
All the labour of man is for his mouth, and yet
the appetite is not filled" (Eccl. 6:6–7).

The Preacher does offer some glimmering
sparks of light in the midst of his dark observations. He writes:

It is good and comely for one to eat and to drink, and to enjoy the good of all his labour that he taketh under the sun all the days of his life, which God giveth him: for it is his portion. Every man also to whom God hath given riches and wealth, and hath given him power to eat thereof, and to take his portion, and to rejoice in his labour; this is the gift of God. For he shall not much remember the days of his life; because God answereth him in the joy of his heart (Eccl. 5:18–20).

Note the difference here between a person who greedily pursues wealth and one who finds enjoyment in work. The Preacher says the one enjoys his labor because he sees it as a gift of God. Moreover, God gives him joy in his heart so that he does not remember the toil of labor as much as contentment in his covenant Lord.

Where Wisdom Finds Contentment

The Preacher's observations on greed are developed further in the New Testament. Jesus says, "No man can serve two masters: for either he will hate the one, and love the other; or else he will hold to the one, and despise the other. Ye cannot serve God and mammon" (Matt. 6:24). The heart of this statement is that greed is idolatry. The apostle Paul makes this abundantly clear when he says, "Mortify therefore your members which are upon the earth; fornication, uncleanness, inordinate affection, evil concupiscence, and covetousness, which is idolatry" (Col. 3:5).

Part of the problem with greed is that it, like a number of other sins within the church, is so difficult to identify. We easily condemn sins such as drunkenness or homosexuality, yet we are not so quick to point the finger at idolatry, or greed and covetousness, which cut across all financial and social classes. What do our lifestyles say about our devotion to Christ? We should be brutally honest with ourselves. Do we seek fleeting satisfaction in wealth and possessions, or do we find genuine joy in the labor that God gives us?

If we look for satisfaction in things rather than God's blessings in Christ through the Spirit, we see the depth of the problem. Rather than comparing ourselves to our neighbors, we must gaze into the mirror of the Law until we recognize that regardless of our possessions, greed is ultimately a motive of our heart. If we are honest, we will recognize our greed as wickedness and idolatry. Only the Spirit of God can help us recognize our greed. We might rid ourselves of many possessions, and from all appearances, live a modest life. However, only Christ through the Spirit can change what's in our heart. For this reason Paul writes in Colossians 3:1–4:

> If ye then be risen with Christ, seek those things which are above, where Christ sitteth on the right hand of God. Set your affection

on things above, not on things on the earth. For ye are dead, and your life is hid with Christ in God. When Christ, who is our life, shall appear, then shall ye also appear with him in glory.

Only in seeking Christ will we find joy, contentment, and satisfaction. Paul must have had Christ's teaching in mind when he wrote Colossians 3, for Jesus makes the same point:

Lay not up for yourselves treasures upon earth, where moth and rust doth corrupt, and where thieves break through and steal: but lay up for yourselves treasures in heaven, where neither moth nor rust doth corrupt, and where thieves do not break through nor steal: for where your treasure is, there will your heart be also (Matt. 6:19–21).

Elsewhere Paul echoes the sentiments of the Preacher when he speaks of contentment:

But godliness with contentment is great gain. For we brought nothing into this world, and it is certain we can carry nothing out. And having food and raiment let us be therewith content. But they that will be rich fall into temptation and a snare, and into many foolish and hurtful lusts, which drown men in destruction and perdition. For the love of money is the root of all evil: which while some coveted after, they have erred from the faith, and pierced themselves through with many sorrows (1 Tim. 6:6–10).

We should ask ourselves every day where we find our contentment and joy. Before buying something, we should ask whether we expect to find contentment in it. This does not mean we should never buy anything; rather, like Scripture says, we should address the motives of our heart in all we do.

Nor is this an indictment against wealth. Abraham was a very wealthy man, yet the author of Hebrews tells us: "By faith he sojourned in the land of promise, as in a strange country, dwelling in tabernacles with Isaac and Jacob, the heirs with him of the same promise: for he looked for a city which hath foundations, whose builder and maker is God" (Heb. 11:9–10). Abraham looked beyond wealth; for he sought the kind of contentment that can only be found in Christ.

When you consider a new job opportunity, will your chief concern be a higher salary or a more prestigious title? If you seek contentment in Christ first, then everything else will be in proper perspective.

An old Puritan prayer describes the nature of a heart that is content in Christ:

> I pray for joy, wait for joy, long for joy; give me more than I can hold, desire, or think of. Measure out to me my times and degrees of joy, at my work, business, duties. If I weep at night, give me joy in the morning. Let me rest in the thought of thy love, pardon for

sin, my title to heaven, my future unspotted state…. Let my heart leap towards the eternal sabbath, where the work of redemption, sanctification, preservation, glorification is finished and perfected forever, where thou wilt rejoice over me with joy ("Joy," in *Valley of Vision*, 162).

Conclusion

True contentment can only be found in Christ. Only when we are content in Christ will we enjoy food and drink and toil, seeing them as gifts from God. Only when we are content in Christ will we focus less on the days of our toil because God has occupied our hearts with joy.

STUDY QUESTIONS

1. Why is the pursuit of wealth and posses-
sions vanity? *It all fades; you can't take anything w/ you when you die and it can't be idolatry*

2. How is labor a gift from God?
The ability to work is a gift; a job is a gift. - God provides through our labor.

3. How do we find true contentment in
Christ? *We were created by Him, for Him to be in a relationship w/ Him. without Him we can't be content because*

4. Is the possession of wealth automatically
sinful? Why not? *no, it is the love of these things that lead to idolatry*

5. How is greed idolatry?
We trust and worship in something other than God.

We are going against the very nature of how we were created

8
Wisdom and Folly

Read Ecclesiastes 6:10–7:14

The Preacher has taught us about the vanity of wealth, greed in particular. He has observed the futility of pursuing wealth, for as the apostle Paul also taught, we come into the world with nothing and leave with nothing. But it is possible to find enjoyment in a simple meal and drink or even in toilsome labor if we recognize that everything is a gift from God. Ultimately we will not find contentment in things but only in a person, Jesus Christ.

The Preacher now moves from observations to a number of pithy proverbs. He does this to contrast wisdom and folly. Some of these proverbs are quite odd and appear pessimistic. In the end, however, the Preacher shows us that the wisdom of God far surpasses the folly and wisdom of man. The pinnacle of God's wisdom is Jesus Christ,

God's only begotten Son. Ultimately the Preacher says we must yearn to possess the mind of Christ.

The Pities of Life

The Preacher begins the seventh chapter with something expected but ends with something unexpected. He begins by saying, "A good name is better than precious ointment" (Eccl. 7:1). We understand the importance of having a good name, for one's reputation is crucial. It is more desirous than precious ointment, which doesn't refer to some lotion we might buy at a drugstore, but to something like myrrh, which was extremely expensive in the ancient world.

We can understand the first part of verse 1, but what about the last part, which says the day of death is better than the day of one's birth? To understand, we must remember that the Preacher is contrasting wisdom and folly here. So we should ask in what way we can learn more about wisdom from death than we can from birth.

The day of birth is so filled with joy and excitement that we can forget many of our troubles as we gaze into the eyes of a baby. The day of death is entirely different. It is filled with sadness, yes, but it also prompts deep reflection on the significance of life, its fragility, and its temporary nature. For the Christian, it is also a time for contemplating ultimate questions, such as, why must people die? What happens to people after they die? Scripture answers these questions, telling us we die because we have sinned and have brought death upon us. There is life after death, but whether we have an afterlife of blessing or curse is another matter. These observations may have led the Preacher to write: "It is better to go to the house of mourning, than to go to the house of feasting: for that is the end of all men; and the living will lay it to his heart. Sorrow is better than laughter: for by the sadness of the countenance the heart is made better" (Eccl. 7:2–3). If we seek wisdom, we can more likely find it at a funeral than at a party.

Mourning offers time for reflection and soul-searching, whereas a party prompts light and airy conversation and may go no deeper than to ask, is there more guacamole? I like a party as much as anyone, but it is hardly a place to find wisdom. The Preacher makes this point when he says, "The heart of the wise is in the house of mourning; but the heart of fools is in the house of mirth. It is better to hear the rebuke of the wise, than for a man to hear the song of fools. For as the crackling of thorns under a pot, so is the laughter of the fool: this also is vanity" (Eccl. 7:4–6). A fool may have fun and be the life of a party, but in the end, his laughter is futility.

From here, the Preacher shifts to reflect on what is better: the beginning or the end of a thing. In verse 8 he tells us that the end of a thing is better than the beginning, and that patience is better than pride. He goes on to say that it is better to be patient than to give way to quick-tempered anger, for anger lodges in the bosom of fools.

How many horrible things have happened as the result of rage? How many people have been convicted of murder after a fit of rage? How many wives have been beaten by husbands with a short fuse? How many children have been injured by short-tempered parents? Notice how the Preacher's statements about patience fit with his proverbs about the superiority of death over birth and mourning over laughter. At a certain point, a person may lack the patience to endure a difficult period or time of mourning. Such a person might be angry about the turn of events in his life and long for days gone by.

The Preacher says to such a person, "Say not thou, What is the cause that the former days were better than these? for thou dost not inquire wisely concerning this" (Eccl. 7:10). The wise man recognizes that there is an ebb and flow to life, and one experiences both times of joy and sorrow. What lies behind this statement is stated at the end of chapter 6: "That which hath been is named already, and it is known that it is man: neither may he contend with him that is mightier than he. Seeing there be many things that increase vanity, what is man the better?" (Eccl. 6:10–11). The point is there is nothing new under the sun, including the ebb and flow of life.

Though we might argue with God about how He ordains things, the effort is futile, the Preacher says. Who can win a debate with God? The more words we utter in such a context, the more futile our efforts become. They are of no advantage, for they are like spitting in the wind. Realizing this does not give way to the kind of fatalism Doris Day sang about: "Que será será, whatever will be, will be, the future's not ours to see, Que será será."

Rather, the wise man recognizes that in the ebb and flow of life he must acknowledge the Preacher's words: "In the day of prosperity be joyful, but in the day of adversity consider: God also hath set the one over against the other, to the end that man should find nothing after him" (Eccl. 7:14). In many ways these words echo what the Preacher says about toil: it is a gift of God, and in recognizing it as such, the wise man is filled with joy. So too, the wise man recognizes that in the ebb and flow of life, joy and sorrow come from God. But there is more.

All Things through Christ

Ecclesiastes is part of a greater story. It is incomplete apart from Christ and the New Testament. The wise man inherently knows that God is not capricious and does not play with His creatures as if they were disposable. In the world where we live, death is certainly present, but it exists because man willfully sinned against the command of God. We have earned God's wrath and condemnation for our sin. But God has shown us mercy in His Son by redeeming us from our rebellion and wickedness.

Jesus Christ, the Son of God, is the embodiment of wisdom. The apostle Paul says God has made Christ our wisdom, righteousness, sanctification, and redemption (1 Cor. 1:30). All the treasures of wisdom and knowledge are hidden in Christ (Col. 2:3). When the Preacher contrasts wisdom and folly, he is ultimately contrasting the mind of Christ with the wisdom of the world, which in the end is folly.

In Christ we realize that we have brought sorrow and death upon ourselves because of our willful rejection of God's authority. We recognize that we suffer the just consequences of our disobedience. However, when we repent and are joined to Christ by Spirit-wrought, God-given faith, our eyes are opened to the wisdom of God in Christ. We now see the difference between wisdom and folly. We also are comforted that the seemingly aimless ebb and flow of life is not random nor is simply the consequences of our sin. At certain times in our lives, we do suffer the consequences of our sin. However, the Preacher is not referring to those times here but to the seemingly meaningless suffering that the righteous endure.

In Christ, we realize that in the ebb and flow of life, joy and sorrow, birth and death are the crucible God uses to conform us to the image of His Son. For Christians, suffering is never pointless. Paul thus could assure the church in Rome that all things work together for the good of those who love God and are called according to His purpose (Rom. 8:28–32). As we receive the mind of Christ through the work of the Spirit, we recognize the truth that death is better than birth, and mourning is better than laughter. We are not sadists who simply surrender to the darkness of night. Rather, in the face of death, we so see our sinfulness, finitude, fragility, and uncertainty of life that we can only cling to Christ, knowing that He has conquered death. We cry out with the apostle Paul:

> O death, where is thy sting? O grave, where is thy victory? The sting of death is sin; and the strength of sin is the law. But thanks be to God, which giveth us the victory through our Lord Jesus Christ. Therefore, my beloved brethren, be ye stedfast, unmoveable, always abounding in the work of the Lord, forasmuch as ye know that your labour is not in vain in the Lord (1 Cor. 15:55–58).

As we face death, we see that mourning is better than laughter, because the fool says in his heart that there is no God. He goes off to party, laughing like the crackling of thorns under a pot. But sadly, his laughter soon gives way to mourning as he eventually discovers that he has spurned true wisdom, Jesus Christ, and will suffer eternal, just condemnation for it. In Greek theater, the lot of the fool is a tragedy, for his story always ends in his downfall.

Ironically the fool does not go into the night screaming in defiance but rather with a cocktail in his hand as he toasts his eternal damnation with laughter. The wise man, who may find himself surrounded by darkness, mourning, and even intense suffering, belongs to Christ and thus has a different outlook. In Christ, the wise man overcomes adversity. His story ends in joy. For us who are united to Christ by faith through the Spirit, everything that happens to us is used by God for His glory and to conform us to the image of His Son. Life is no longer a tragedy but rather the school of Christ in which we learn wisdom. We know that one day death will give way to life, and mourning will give way to joy. Our joy is not fleeting, nor is it laughter in the face of fate. Rather, it is the everlasting joy and happiness that is grounded upon God's love in Christ.

Conclusion
In Christ we may rejoice in days of prosperity as well as in days of adversity, for God has made both. Both bring glory to Him and conform us to the image of Christ. Pray, therefore, for the mind of Christ that we might view these things with wisdom, not foolishness.

STUDY QUESTIONS

1. How is death better than life? *It causes us to comtemplate, soul search our own afterlife, where we are in Christ*

2. Are times of joy as well as suffering from the hand of God? How is that so? *Yes It is the ebb and flow of life*

3. What is the ultimate goal of times of joy and sorrow? *When we recognize that joy and sorrow comes from God, we will have peace, contentment and joy.*

4. How are we enabled to see that both times of joy and sorrow are a gift from God?

Through the Holy Spirit

To ultimately conform us into the image of His Son.

9
Is No One Righteous?

Read Ecclesiastes 7:15–29

In the previous chapter, the Preacher contrasted wisdom and folly, offering many pithy proverbs to teach us that mourning is better than laughter and the day of death better than the day of birth. In this, the Preacher was not a pessimist or sadist. Rather, he wanted us to recognize that all things, whether joy or adversity, are from God, who uses everything that happens to us to conform us to the image of His Son.

The Preacher now continues his contrast of wisdom and folly in other ways. At first glance, some of his observations sound odd and perhaps even ungodly. However, as we examine what he says, we will see that the Preacher is pointing us in a specific direction. In the midst of life's uncertainties and the mystery of some of life's greatest questions, the Preacher tells us to fear God. In the midst of darkness, he offers us a glimmer of hope that eventually gives way to the dawn of the revelation of God in Christ.

Is Anyone Righteous?

In the beginning of this section, the Preacher compares wisdom and folly by noting an apparent difference between the two:

> All things have I seen in the days of my vanity: there is a just man that perisheth in his righteousness, and there is a wicked man that prolongeth his life in his wickedness. Be not righteous over much; neither make thyself over wise: why shouldest thou destroy thyself? Be not over much wicked, neither be thou foolish: why shouldest thou die before thy time (Eccl. 7:15–17)?

Though it seems right that the righteous should outlive the wicked, the reverse is more often true. Certainly we have noted in our lifetime the truism that only the good die young. We hear stories of heroism and bravery from the frontlines of war, where young men sacrifice themselves to protect fellow soldiers. Many medals of honor have been awarded for such bravery. At the same time, we know that many murderers run loose and criminals live unchecked in their evil.

What is the answer to this apparent inequity? If you are too noble or too righteous, will you die sooner rather than later? If so, should you refrain from being too righteous? On the other hand, if you are too wicked, this opens you up to possible retribution from the authorities or the judgment of God. So should you seek the middle ground, not being too righteous or too wicked, so you may live a long life?

If we ask people on the street or even in the church whether they are worthy of eternal life, most would refrain from making an outright claim on eternal life. They might say, "I've done some bad things, but I'm not that bad, and I've tried to live a good life, though I'm not that good."

That is not what the Preacher says. He seeks wisdom that meditates upon the Law of God day and night and comes to the following conclusion: "For there is not a just man upon earth, that doeth good, and sinneth not" (Eccl. 7:20). No matter how righteous a person is, all people sin. If all people sin, then all are liable to God's just punishment. The psalmist makes the same observation as the Preacher in saying, "Enter not into judgment with thy servant: for in thy sight shall no man living be justified" (Ps. 143:2).

What is the answer to this apparent theological dilemma? How should we live if we are not to seek the middle ground between good and evil? The Preacher's response is: "It is good that thou shouldest take hold of this; yea, also from this withdraw not thine hand: for he that feareth God

shall come forth of them all. Wisdom strength-
eneth the wise more than ten mighty men which
are in the city" (Eccl. 7:18–19). The Preacher says
the answer to life is not found within man but
outside of him—in fear of the Lord. The answer
is not looking inward but looking outward. This
kind of wisdom gives strength to the wise "more
than ten mighty men which are in the city."

The Preacher, however, is not done. To show
that the answer to his theological puzzle is not
found within man, the Preacher makes some
observations. To amplify what he has said in verse
20 that there is not a righteous man on earth who
does good and never sins, he offers some illustra-
tions in verses 21–22. He says a person should
not take too seriously everything that people say,
lest he hears his servant cursing him. He says this
because if we are honest with ourselves, we will
recognize that we have thought ill of many in our
lives, perhaps in private. We may also have said
evil things about others, no matter how politely.
Later we realize that we have spoken wrongly
or even sinned in speaking ill of others. In other
words, there is not a righteous man on earth who
always does good and never sins!

The Preacher tested his conclusions by con-
ducting a search. He wanted to make himself wise
by observing the wickedness of folly and the foolishness that is madness (v. 25). But the Preacher
found something more bitter than death. He

says, "I find more bitter than death the woman, whose heart is snares and nets, and her hands as bands: whoso pleaseth God shall escape from her; but the sinner shall be taken by her" (Eccl. 7:26). He found the wicked woman whom the author of Proverbs describes as death: "For the lips of a strange woman drop as an honeycomb, and her mouth is smoother than oil: but her end is bitter as wormwood, sharp as a two edged sword. Her feet go down to death; her steps take hold on hell" (Prov. 5:3–5).

The Preacher sees the wicked woman and notes that the person who pleases God escapes her, but the wicked man falls into her trap. We might thus think, "Aha! The righteous escape death, right?" The Preacher dismisses that assumption. He says, "Behold, this have I found…counting one by one, to find out the account: which yet my soul seeketh, but I find not: one man among a thousand have I found; but a woman among all those have I not found" (Eccl. 7:27–28).

These two verses seem difficult to understand, but let us press on. First, we must remember that the Preacher is on a quest to see if anyone can escape death. He is testing the theory that the righteous die but the wicked live. He is asking whether anyone may avoid death. He has just shown that the wicked die, for the wanton woman lures them into her bed, but her feet lead straight to Sheol—to death. As for the righteous, the Preacher discovers that 99.9 percent of all men die, and 100 percent of all women. The phrase *one out of a thousand* is a biblical colloquialism for *one out of all men* (Job 33:23). In other words, of all the men who have lived, the Preacher only found .1 percent who did not die.

Who in the Old Testament did not die? Enoch did not die but was carried to heaven as he walked with God. Elijah is another exception to the general rule that all people die. No women in the Old Testament escaped death. So the Preacher concludes that the wicked are swept away by death, but so are the righteous. That conclusion gives the Preacher pause, though he goes on to conclude what he knows for sure: "Lo, this only have I found, that God hath made man upright; but they have sought out many inventions" (Eccl. 7:29). Contrast verse 29 with the end of verse 28 to see that the Preacher found that God made man upright, but man sinned and ever since has tried many schemes to avoid death, but to no avail. In short, all men sin and are subject to death.

The Only Righteous Man

Man is incapable of saving himself from death, the Preacher says. The apostle Paul also makes this same observation, saying, "For the wages of sin is death" (Rom. 6:23). Paul also quotes the psalmist when he says, "As it is written, There is none righteous, no, not one: there is none that understandeth, there is none that seeketh after God. They are all gone out of the way, they are together become unprofitable; there is none that doeth good, no, not one…. There is no fear of God before their eyes" (Rom. 3:10–18). Notice that the unbeliever does not fear God, which is the exact opposite of what the Preacher says of the righteous man (v. 18). The answer to man's predicament of his sin-fallen condition and its consequence, death, are not within him. The answer, according to the Preacher, is fear of God.

In the antiphonal exchange of the Old and New Testaments, we find Paul answering the question "What is fear of God?" of the Preacher and the psalmist (Ps. 143:2) by saying, "Knowing that a man is not justified by the works of the law, but by the faith of Jesus Christ, even we have believed in Jesus Christ, that we might be justified by the faith of Christ, and not by the works of the law: for by the works of the law shall no flesh be justified" (Gal. 2:16). The answer to the Preacher's quest is the fear of God, specifically through faith in Christ. Indeed, Christ is the only person who was completely righteous and did not sin. Christ has also suffered and died on our behalf.

The assumptions of Enoch and Elijah, who did not see death, find their fulfillment in Christ's resurrection from the dead. Jesus is not a rare exception to the rule of death. Rather, by offering a perfect sacrifice and living in perfect obedience to God, He fulfilled the Law and now becomes the example of all who look to Him by faith. Only through faith in Christ, who lived, died, resurrected, and ascended to God, are we able to escape the clutches of eternal death. More importantly, only because Christ suffered the wrath of God on our behalf may we escape the eternal wrath of God that is justly ours. Paul thus says, "For what the law could not do, in that it was weak through the flesh, God sending his own Son in the likeness of sinful flesh, and for sin, condemned sin in the flesh" (Rom. 8:3).

So death must come to us all because we all have sinned and are guilty before God. We must therefore repent of our sin and look to Jesus by faith, trusting what He has done on our behalf. Even as Christians, we may sometimes be overwhelmed by our fierce enemy, death. In many respects, this fierce enemy led the Preacher on his quest to find answers. But whether we face our own demise or the death of a loved one, we are not without hope. We die because we sin, but we live because Jesus has died in our place and has been raised from the dead.

Conclusion

We may all die one day, regardless of our own efforts. But we will live after death if we have faith in the One whom God has sent to deliver us from the curse of the Law and the eternal consequences of our sin. As Romans 8:11 assures us, "But if the Spirit of him that raised up Jesus from the dead dwell in you, he that raised up Christ from the dead shall also quicken your mortal bodies by his Spirit that dwelleth in you."

STUDY QUESTIONS

1. Since both the wicked and the righteous die, do both have the same end? *Those in Christ escape eternal death because of what He has done.*

2. In the Old Testament, who are the only exceptions to the rule that all people die? *Enoch, Elijah*

3. What hope does the resurrection of Christ give to believers in the face of death? *We will also be resurrected and live with Him*

4. Is man's escape from death found within or without himself? *Without —ONLY through Christ*

10
Fearing the King

Read Ecclesiastes 8:1–17

In contrasting wisdom and folly in the previous chapter, the Preacher observes that the wicked appear to outlive the righteous. He goes on a quest to see if that is true and if there is a way for man to prolong his life and to live eternally. He finds that of all people, only Enoch and Elijah have escaped death. The answer, then, to a long life is not within man, but outside of him. The only way to live long, even eternally, is for man to look outside of himself and to trust in God, specifically in the person of Christ. Through Christ's life, death, resurrection, and ascension, we can have the forgiveness of sins and escape the consequences of sin, which include eternal death.

Now the Preacher explores what it means to fear God. In using those words, the Bible does not mean what John Calvin called a "servile fear" but rather an attitude of respect and honor. Fearing God can be difficult at times, given what we observe in the world, the Preacher says. Yet even in the midst of injustice and things that we do not understand, we must fear God.

The Preacher does not advocate blind faith or a fatalistic acceptance of everything that happens to us, for God has not called us to anything that He has not already accomplished through His Son, Jesus. Thus we will see that even in the uncertainties of life, we can take shelter beneath the mighty wings of Christ.

The Nature of Godly Fear

The Preacher offers his observations in three sections, which we can explain under the following headings: obey the king (vv. 1–9); fear God and do well (vv. 10–13); and God's inscrutable ways (vv. 14–17). Let us go to the first set of observations.

1. *Obey the King* (vv. 1–9)

The Preacher begins by asking: "Who is as the wise man? and who knoweth the interpretation of a thing? a man's wisdom maketh his face to shine, and the boldness of his face shall be changed" (Eccl. 8:1). This brings to mind two of Israel's greatest men, Joseph and Daniel. Both were wise men, and both interpreted dreams for their kings. In the interpretation of these dreams, both revealed the wisdom of God and helped their kings by navigating difficult matters. Joseph interpreted Pharaoh's dream warning of a coming famine, prepared the Egyptians for the food shortage, and allowed them to survive, even providing shelter for the Israelites. Daniel interpreted Nebuchadnezzar's dream, which allowed the king to see the kingdoms that would come after him, and though in very shadowy terms, gave him a glimpse of the kingdom of the coming Messiah, which would rule over every other kingdom.

These wise men exemplified the counsel the Preacher offers to his readers, namely, keeping the king's command. The Preacher is not saying we should in every circumstance do what our ruler commands. Scripture itself offers some exceptions to this rule. For example, Daniel and his three friends refused to worship Nebuchadnezzar's idol. Daniel also refused to obey the king's orders to stop praying to God and was thrown into a lion's den. Nevertheless, the Preacher tells us: "Whoso keepeth the commandment shall feel no evil thing: and a wise man's heart discerneth both time and judgment. Because to every purpose there is time and judgment, therefore the misery of man is great upon him" (Eccl. 8:5–6). The Preacher says a wise man will know when he should disobey the king. Generally, however, he will submit to the king's authority.

The Preacher advises us to "keep the king's commandment," because as Paul later says in Romans 13, all authority is established by God, even the authority of a king. Many Christians seem to forget this. Our political allegiance is often driven by whether we like the one in authority or whether he meets our needs. Perhaps this attitude is rooted in the history of our nation, which was conceived in rebellion to authority. Nevertheless, we should ask ourselves whether we have allowed our American democratic ideals to color our reading of the Scriptures. What counsel might we give to a Christian who lives under a government that is less than democratic: Rebellion? Subterfuge? Disrespect? The answer is none of these, the Preacher says. The answer is to keep the king's command.

Like Daniel, who faithfully served Nebuchadnezzar who was unrighteous most of his life, we too are called to obey those in authority. Christ Himself exemplified this attitude. When religious leaders tried to trick Jesus into a revolutionary statement that they could use against Him, Jesus told His interrogators to render unto Caesar what is Caesar's, and unto God what belongs to God. Jesus even submitted to ungodly rulers as He was led to His crucifixion. He could have called upon legions of angels to deliver Him, but He did not. The Preacher's next observation tells us why.

2. *Fear God and Do Well* (vv. 10–13)

The Preacher has noted how the wicked seem to go on unchecked in doing evil as though they can prolong their life by doing so. He is especially sickened by seeing that when a wicked man is buried, he is praised by people in the temple and in the city as if he were a saint. It is one thing for a wicked man to go unchecked in evil and to live a long life. However, it is worse to see the wicked baptized in the water of praise by people in the church.

For example, the German churches endorsed the Nazi regime in the early 1930s by agreeing to the so-called Führer's principle, which required all preachers to be "politically reliable and offer no criticism of the Reich; accept the superiority of the Aryan race; expel Jewish Christians from the ranks of the clergy; and acknowledge that Hitler was lord over the German church." Many Protestant churches in Germany opposed this principle in the Barmen Declaration, which affirmed that Christ alone was the head of the church. But lest we think ourselves immune to endorsing evil in our own land, we should remember that today many churches invite politicians from both the left and right to speak about their views, whether those are God-honoring or not.

The Preacher might have given up after seeing the injustice of good people affirming evil. Yet he does not. He says, "Though a sinner do evil an hundred times, and his days be prolonged, yet surely I know that it shall be well with them that fear God, which fear before him: but it shall not be well with the wicked, neither shall he prolong his days, which are as a shadow; because he feareth not before God" (Eccl. 8:12–13). Rather than giving up, the Preacher entrusts himself to the Lord. Though wicked people do great evil, which is endorsed by the church, the Preacher knows that in the end, the Lord will right all wrongs.

We find this type of trust in Christ in the midst of His great suffering. The author of Hebrews says about Christ in agony in the garden of Gethsemane: "When he had offered up prayers and supplications with strong crying and tears unto him that was able to save him from death, and was heard in that he feared; though he were a Son, yet learned he obedience by the things which he suffered" (Heb. 5:7–8). Even when faced with death at the hands of unjust authorities, Jesus entrusted Himself to the hands of His heavenly Father. In the depths of His suffering, He embodied the statement of Job: "Though he slay me, yet will I trust in him" (Job 13:15). In the worst moments of His suffering, when He said, "My God, my God, why hast thou forsaken me?" (Mark 15:34), Christ knew that the wicked would not prevail. Though it seemed that God did not hear His Son's cries, He answered His Son three days later by raising Christ from the dead. He thereby reversed the unjust verdict that had been passed against Christ. Moreover, God the Father then seated His Son at His right hand from which He would rule the nations.

3. *God's Inscrutable Ways* (vv. 14–17)

The Preacher once again addresses the dilemma that the righteous appear to receive the reward of the wicked, and the wicked receive the reward of the righteous. The Preacher tells us:

> When I applied mine heart to know wisdom, and to see the business that is done upon the earth: (for also there is that neither day nor night seeth sleep with his eyes:) then I beheld all the work of God, that a man cannot find out the work that is done under the sun: because though a man labour to seek it out, yet he shall not find it; yea further; though a wise man think to know it, yet shall he not be able to find it (Eccl. 8:16–17).

There are no pat answers for this dilemma, the Preacher says, for often we are left with more questions than answers. Sometimes when we look back on a time of trial or difficulty in our life, we can see how God used that for our profit. Yet other times hindsight offers us little or no insight. Then we must simply trust that our heavenly Father has our best interests at heart. He has not designed evil for us nor has He forgotten us.

Christ tells us that when we ask for bread, our heavenly Father does not give us a stone or a ser-

pent but cares for our every need. The Preacher
anticipates Christ's statement in saying: "Then I
commended mirth, because a man hath no better
thing under the sun, than to eat, and to drink, and
to be merry: for that shall abide with him of his
labour the days of his life, which God giveth him
under the sun" (Eccl. 8:15). Yet we must remember that God does not sit aloof on His throne
while musing about His suffering creatures. On
the contrary, we must contemplate who God is by
looking at the cross, where God has revealed Himself in the crucified Messiah.

Seeing God through the crucified Christ reminds
us of two crucial truths. First, if we think of God
apart from the cross, we might think that the
cause of our suffering lies outside of ourselves. We
might see ourselves as victims of evil. But when we
see God through the crucified Christ, we are confronted with our sin. We see we are not victims of
evil but agents of it. We brought sin into the world
by our disobedience, first through the rebellion of
our first parents in the Garden of Eden. Then their
disobedience became our disobedience (Rom. 5:12).
As the Preacher says in Ecclesiastes 7:20, "There is
not a just man upon earth, that doeth good, and
sinneth not," and in 7:29, "Lo, this only have I
found, that God hath made man upright; but they
have sought out many inventions."

Second, by seeing God through the cross, we
will realize how He condescended to us, His sin-

ful and rebellious creatures, by sending His Son, Jesus Christ, into this sin-fallen world to suffer throughout His life and to be crucified for us so we might live. Christ does not merely show us the way by His example of righteousness, but indeed secures righteousness for us who are by nature children of wrath and God's enemies. If we view our lives through the cross of Christ, we will also see the world and our existence in a different light. We will recognize that we are redeemed and live by God's grace. We will be able to take pleasure in something as simple as a meal, seeing it as a divine blessing.

In suffering great trials or injustice, we will humbly submit to God's hand of Providence, knowing that we do not have to search for answers but rather, like Christ, may entrust ourselves to the Lord's care. We do so, not blindly or as if reaching for something to dull our pain, but rather in the knowledge that the God-man has entered into our suffering to redeem and transform us. But take note: the Preacher says man will not find out the work of God that is done *under the sun* (v. 17). This phrase, which is one of the Preacher's favorites, refers to man's sin-fallen condition. A synonymous phrase, *under the heaven(s)*, is used in Genesis 6 in reference to the flood. The point is that today we must live by faith in Christ, trusting in the Providence of our heavenly Father.

One day that faith will give way to sight. One day the seemingly confusing, disparate, and unintelligible threads of history will be revealed as a grand tapestry that tells the story of God's glory in Christ through the lives of His people in their triumphs and losses, their joys and their sorrows. All of our questions will be answered as we behold the face of God in Christ. We at last will know as we are known.

Conclusion

The Preacher's message is simple: we must at all times and in every situation trust our heavenly Father. We have every reason to do so, for He has given us the Lord Jesus, who has redeemed us from our sin-fallen condition through His life, death, resurrection, and ascension. Yet only through God's Spirit-wrought grace may we have faith in Christ and trust in our heavenly Father's providential care. We must pray that He will enlarge our faith and trust so that we may see everything in our lives—our victories and defeats, our joys and our sorrows—through the cross of Christ.

STUDY QUESTIONS

1. Why must we obey people who rule over us? *Because God sets up those in authority*

2. How has God submitted to His own providence? *By taking on flesh – Jesus Christ.*

3. Why must Christians who suffer under unjust authority submit to their rulers? *Because Christ did the very same same*

4. What does the cross of Christ teach us about submitting to unjust authority? *Obedience, trust in the Father's plan for us.*

11
Death Comes to All

Read Ecclesiastes 9:1–10

The Preacher has instructed us in three related matters. First, we should obey the king's command, not in fear of man but in fear of God, for God has ordained all authority. Second, those who fear God will do well, and those who do not fear God will encounter God's just judgment. Third, we cannot know God's ways. In these three seemingly disparate observations, the Preacher teaches us that even during life's greatest challenges and trials, we must trust in God's providential care. We should not view God as one who is aloof from our suffering. Rather, any time we think about God, we must see Him as He revealed Himself in the crucified Messiah. In the cross we see that God in the flesh has submitted Himself to His own providence to deliver us from our sin and death.

Throughout our whole lives, then, we must stay in the shadow of the cross as we follow in Christ's footsteps and are conformed to His image.

Now the Preacher addresses the subject of death, which in one sense, is the ultimate trial for man. The Preacher and people who are approaching death know that death is the great equalizer. No matter how we try, we cannot escape death. No matter how wealthy or poor a person is, how righteous or wicked, he will die, for death waits for no one. In view of this end, the Preacher offers a message of hope that will find ultimate fulfillment in Jesus Christ.

Thoughts on Life and Death

The Preacher says death comes to all people, whether they love or hate, are righteous or wicked, good or evil, clean or unclean, offer sacrifices or not, shun an oath or take one. The apparent injustice of this is obvious. How can a just God treat everyone alike in death regardless of how they lived? Furthermore, is the Preacher suggesting that we should simply cave in to the inevitable and end life?

The existentialist philosopher Jean-Paul Sartre thought so. He said that since he had appeared by chance, he therefore had no right to exist. He once berated his friends for eating and drinking to preserve their existence when in the end they had no reason to exist. Sartre proposed suicide as the only legitimate response to life, given that God did not exist, for ending one's life was the only meaningful thing a person could do to authenticate his existence.

The famous philosopher Friedrich Nietzsche responded a bit differently to the inevitability of death. In his book *The Gay Science*, Nietzsche heralds the death of God. He tells people around him that they have all killed God. The only sound they hear now is the noise of gravediggers preparing to entomb God in the earth. Nietzsche's response to death is to be an *übermench*, or *superman*, who carves out his own existence, spits in the face of all religion, and defines his own morals and ethics. He says a superman will overcome the trials of life by his sheer will to live.

If Sartre and Nietzsche were on the Titanic, Sartre would see the waters surrounding the sinking ship and would consider ending his life. He would sit on the deck of the ship, drink a cup of tea, put a gun to his head, and pull the trigger, not because he feared drowning but because he had no right to live, even for a few more moments. Nitezsche, on the other hand, would stand upon the bow of the ship, raise his fist into the air, and spit at death. The problem is that both Sartre and Nietzsche would die, regardless of their attitude, for death is inevitable for all.

The Preacher does not give us such advice, even when confronted with inevitable death. He still has hope. This hope, however, is not Pollyanna-like; it does not say everything will be okay if we just hope. The Preacher tells us that life, even in the smallest way, is better than death:

> For to him that is joined to all the living there is hope: for a living dog is better than a dead lion. For the living know that they shall die: but the dead know not any thing, neither have they any more a reward; for the memory of them is forgotten. Also their love, and their hatred, and their envy, is now perished; neither have they any more a portion for ever in any thing that is done under the sun" (Eccl. 9:4–6).

Some philosophers, like Sartre, might say the Preacher is sticking his head in the sand like an ostrich that refuses to deal with reality. On the other hand, people like Nietzsche might consider such a response weak in scrounging whatever scraps of life one can find. But this is far from the truth.

The Preacher has already observed: "I know that there is no good in them, but for a man to rejoice, and to do good in his life. And also that every man should eat and drink, and enjoy the good of all his labour, it is the gift of God.... I said in mine heart, God shall judge the righteous and the wicked: for there is a time there for every purpose and for every work" (Eccl. 3:11–12, 17). The Preacher knows that life is better than death, and that in light of the faithfulness of God, he can live life to its fullest because it is a gift of God. We can live our lives with joy, for the Preacher says, "Go thy way, eat thy bread with joy, and drink thy wine with a merry heart; for God now accepteth thy works" (Eccl. 9:7). The next verse amplifies this idea: "Let thy garments be always white; and let thy head lack no ointment" (Eccl. 9:8). The Preacher tells us to change our clothing frequently, not merely that we should wear clean clothing but that we should put on garments of joy and celebration. For example, Mordecai, Esther's uncle, changed his everyday clothes to put on a royal robe in celebration of the king's edict allowing the Jews to defend themselves against Haman's wicked plot (Esther 8:15). People in mourning would not change their clothes or anoint themselves with oil (2 Sam. 14:2). The Preacher adds these instructions:

> Live joyfully with the wife whom thou lovest all the days of the life of thy vanity, which he hath given thee under the sun, all the days of thy vanity: for that is thy portion in this life, and in thy labour which thou takest under the sun. Whatsoever thy hand findeth to do, do it with thy might; for there is no work, nor device, nor knowledge, nor wisdom, in the grave, whither thou goest (Eccl. 9:10–11).

The Preacher says that if our lives and work are a gift of God, we may enjoy all of our days. In effect, verse 10 says, "We only have one life to live; therefore, live it to its fullest."

Facing Death with Hope

If we connect the Preacher's observations on hope in facing death to the broader witness of Scripture, we will find the full flowering of this hope in the life, death, and resurrection of Jesus Christ. The New Testament clearly teaches that death has come into the world because of our sin. Like the child who plays with matches and starts a fire that engulfs a house, we clearly violated the command of God by handing our authority to Satan and enslaving ourselves to sin. In His justice, God would have condemned us all to eternal death, and we would have been eternally separated from His loving presence. Sartre fails to recognize his own sinfulness in bringing death into the world. So he says, "I've come this far, so I might as well go all the way and end it." Nietzsche also refuses to acknowledge his own sinfulness, but he claims that he was right in doing what he did. What both philosophers fail to acknowledge is that after death, each person must stand in the presence of God and give an account for his every careless word, thought, and deed.

Sartre thought that after death he would float into a nebulous state of nothingness, while

Nietzsche was convinced that he would experience what he had already proclaimed: God was dead. Both were undoubtedly rudely awakened from their philosophical slumber when they died.

The hope that the Preacher promises is merely a shadow of what Paul proclaims in Romans 6:23: "For the wages of sin is death; but the gift of God is eternal life through Jesus Christ our Lord." By faith in Christ we can look at death and know there is something more (1 Cor. 15:20–26). Christ has conquered death through His life of perfect obedience to the Law, His spotless sacrifice, and His resurrection. Moreover, when Paul says that Jesus is the "firstfruits" (1 Cor. 15:20), he is saying that Jesus is the first portion of the resurrection harvest that is ready and eagerly waiting to be brought in from the field. Not only are we forgiven of our sins, but we are also robed in the grandest festival garments of all, the robe of Christ's righteousness, to await Christ's return and the resurrection of the dead, when we shall be clothed in immortality. In this Paul goes beyond the hope of the Preacher in saying:

> O death, where is thy sting? O grave, where is thy victory? The sting of death is sin; and the strength of sin is the law. But thanks be to God, which giveth us the victory through our Lord Jesus Christ. Therefore, my beloved brethren, be ye stedfast, unmoveable, always abounding in the work of the Lord, foras-

much as ye know that your labour is not in
vain in the Lord (1 Cor. 14:55–58).

Notice that our labor is not in vain. If we were
on the deck of the Titanic, we would not simply
succumb to the inevitable nor would we raise our
fist in defiance. We would labor to preserve our
life and the lives of those around us. We would
cry out to the Lord, asking Him to protect and
save us. We would beg people around us to look
to Christ by faith and confess their sins. Sartre
and Nietzsche might regard our behavior as foolishness. But the wisdom of Christ *is* foolishness to
the world. As the ship went down, we might be
rescued or we might drown. But we would not die
without hope, for our hope is fixed upon Christ
and the resurrection from the dead. Through our
weakness in death, the power and wisdom of
God are manifest in Christ in the resurrection of
Christ's glorious body, the church.

Conclusion

In facing death, our final foe, we have the hope
that is anchored in the life, death, resurrection,
and ascension of our Lord and Savior Jesus Christ.
For though we will die, we will also be resurrected, transformed, and glorified. That means we
can live life to the fullest. We may savor every
moment, knowing that, through faith, our sins
are forgiven in Christ Jesus and we have the hope

of resurrection and eternal life. If this is so, why should we squander our lives in bickering, boasting, pride, sin, divisions, sexual immorality, and the like? Let us rather look by faith to the resurrected Christ and be filled with hope.

We may go forth and do the work of the kingdom, celebrating the life that God has given us and praising Him for it. When we do face death, we can do so with hope. As Geerhardus Vos says, "Let us then not linger at the tomb, but turn our faces and stretch our hands upwards into heaven, where our life is hid with him in God, and whence he shall also come again to show himself to us as he did to Mary, to make us speak the last great 'Rabboni,' which will spring to the lips of all the redeemed, when they meet their Savior in the early dawn of that eternal Sabbath that awaits the people of God" (Vos, *Grace and Glory*, 80–81).

STUDY QUESTIONS

1. What is the significance of the phrase *under the sun*? What does it mean to us?

Everything in this sin-stained world.

2. How did Sartre and Nietzsche look at life and death? How did they say we should react to it? *Very negative; as if life does not matter, it ends in nothing-ness*

3. What did both philosophers fail to recognize in their explanation of human existence? *Life w/o Christ is hopeless but in Christ is hope, life, joy peace*

4. How does the resurrection of Christ give the church hope in the face of death? *Knowing that He was raised; He will raise us up also.*

5. How does the resurrection inform our view of life? *We live with eternity in view; we are just passing through.*

12
Wisdom at All Costs

Read Ecclesiastes 9:11–10:7

We have seen that death comes to all people, both righteous and wicked. At first, this seems unjust. But the Preacher is looking at life from the perspective of this world. When he ventures beyond that, he sees there is more to life. One glimmer of hope is that God will indeed judge the wicked, so the righteous should fear God. This hope flowers in the New Testament in the life, death, and resurrection of Christ. In fearing the Lord, we place our faith in Christ, and through Him we receive eternal life. Because of Christ and His conquest of Satan, sin, and death, we can regard the seemingly inconsequential things in life, such as a simple meal, as gifts from God and, even in the face of death, enjoy them to the fullest.

Now the Preacher makes observations about

pursuing wisdom at all costs. We often tell ourselves that if we obey God, life will be beautiful. Some churches teach a health and wealth gospel, which may have its roots in what people believed as early as Bible times. For example, when Jesus' disciples saw a blind man, they asked, "Master, who did sin, this man, or his parents, that he was born blind?" (John 9:1–2). The disciples believed in the simple maxim: sin and you will be punished; obey and all will go well. The man was blind; therefore he must have sinned, they thought. Jesus refuted that. He said neither the blind man nor his parents had sinned. The man was blind so that God's glory might be revealed in him (John 9:3).

That explanation is at the heart of the Preacher's observation that we must pursue wisdom at all costs. He makes three observations in this context: life is unpredictable (vv. 11–12); wisdom is valuable (vv. 13–18); and wisdom has limitations (10:1–7).

1. *Life is Unpredictable* (vv. 11–12)

This passage begins by echoing a previous observation of the Preacher that death spares no man (Eccl. 9:11–12). In addition, life is quite unpredictable. Certainly a number of things are predictable in life: the sun will rise tomorrow; traffic will be heavy in the morning commute; a rock that I drop will fall to the floor. But the Preacher looks beyond such predictability to things that are not so sure.

Do the fastest runners always win a race? Do the strongest soldiers always win the battle? Generally speaking they do, but not always. For example, in the first part of the twentieth century, Germany had the best trained, best equipped, and most effective soldiers. Yet in both World War I and II, the German armies did not win against other countries. Likewise, on paper, things might seem like a sure bet, but in reality life is often unpredictable. Gamblers in Las Vegas count on that unpredictability to make money on long shots.

But the unpredictability of life vexes the Preacher, for it strikes all people, and though he does not explicitly say so, affects the righteous and the wicked alike as well as the wise and the foolish. From man's limited perspective, think of Job. From all appearances, Job should have lived a blessed life, for he did everything right. Yet without warning, nearly everything he owned and loved was taken from him. And disaster did not overcome the man because he had sinned.

2. *Wisdom is Valuable* (vv. 13–18)

We might think the Preacher would go on to say, "What does it matter, then, if I'm wise or foolish? It makes no difference." Yet he does not say this. Instead, he tells the story of a great king who besieged a small and insignificant city. In the city was a poor man who delivered the city by his wisdom. In this we see that the race is not to the strong or the swift, for a vastly superior force is defeated by a poor but wise man. The *Lord of the Rings* trilogy by J. R. R. Tolkein offers a similar illustration of how seemingly insignificant beings can defeat more powerful ones. In the trilogy, the evil King Sauron and his vastly superior armies are ultimately defeated by the small and insignificant hobbits, whose greatest weapon is their wisdom.

The Preacher goes on to say that wisdom is often unnoticed, unappreciated, and unrewarded. In verse 15 the Preacher says, "Now there was found in it a poor wise man, and he by his wisdom delivered the city; yet no man remembered that same poor man" (Eccl. 9:15). The same cycle is repeated time after time in the book of Judges. The Israelites were often attacked by neighboring nations. They would cry out to God to deliver them, and God would raise up a judge to help deliver them. In the wake of victory, however, the people would forget the Lord. Then they would find themselves right back where they started.

The failure to recognize wisdom on the heels of receiving the fruit of wisdom, such as victory over an enemy, does not prevent the Preacher from honoring wisdom, however. He goes on to say, "Then said I, Wisdom is better than strength: nevertheless the poor man's wisdom is despised, and his words are not heard. The words of wise men are heard in quiet more than the cry of him that ruleth among fools" (Eccl. 9:16–17).

The Preacher continually seeks wisdom, which to him is more valuable than anything. At one time God told Solomon that whatever he asked for would be granted. Solomon did not ask for riches, power, or a long life; he asked the Lord for wisdom (2 Chron. 1:11–12). Wisdom is one of the greatest things a person can have.

3. *Wisdom has Limitations* (10:1–7)

Though wisdom is valuable, it has limitations, for the Preacher tells us that it does not take much to discredit wisdom: "Wisdom is better than weapons of war: but one sinner destroyeth much good" (Eccl. 9:18). The Preacher goes on to say: "Dead flies cause the ointment of the apothecary to send forth a stinking savour: so doth a little folly him that is in reputation for wisdom and honour" (Eccl. 10:1). I am not sure if this statement is the source of the proverbial "fly in the ointment," but the point is clear. You can have lots of wisdom, but one minute of folly can outdo it.

For example, a wise man may give in to one moment of weakness, which ends up ruining his life. Thus wisdom must be like the air we breathe; if we stop breathing, we may soon drown in folly. Verse 2 says the wise man is inclined to the right

and the fool to the left. So, wisdom has limitations, for a little folly can outweigh it. Another
limitation of wisdom is that it cannot hide a fool,
for the folly of a fool will always bubble to the
surface. The Preacher says, "Yea also, when he
that is a fool walketh by the way, his wisdom fail-
eth him, and he saith to every one that he is a
fool" (Eccl. 10:3). A fool will always reveal himself, no matter how he tries to hide under a robe
of wisdom.

Verse 6 seems to contradict this by saying it is
better to remain silent and let people think you are
a fool than to open your mouth and confirm it.
Yet, the fool is deaf to such advice. What is more,
the Preacher is not inconsistent in his observations
on wisdom. He does not say that if we pursue wisdom all will be well and we will prosper. He closes
his observations on wisdom by noting the unpredictability of life: "There is an evil which I have
seen under the sun, as an error which proceedeth
from the ruler: Folly is set in great dignity, and
the rich sit in low place. I have seen servants upon
horses, and princes walking as servants upon the
earth" (Eccl. 10:5–7).

Where Wisdom Is Found
As we reflect on the Preacher's observations,
we must not forget what wisdom ultimately is.
Remember, it is not found in a sage old man who
strokes his goatee as he ponders life's ultimate

questions, but in Christ (1 Cor. 1:30; Col. 2:2–3). In the light of Christ we can make sense of the Preacher's observations.

For example, if we return to the disciples' question regarding the blind man about who sinned, the man or his parents, we observe the unpredictability of life that the Preacher sees. In the midst of this sin-fallen world, God reveals His glory, and He does so according to His own wisdom rather than man's. Paul says the Jews demanded signs and the Greeks sought wisdom, but he and the apostles preached Christ crucified, which was a stumbling block to the Jews and foolishness to Gentiles. God's foolishness is greater than all of man's wisdom, Paul says in 1 Corinthians 1:22–29. From man's perspective, life is unpredictable, but from God's perspective, everything is being done according to His plan.

The believer who has found wisdom in Christ knows that his life is in the providential care of His heavenly Father. So whether he experiences joy or sorrow, he will never be forgotten by his heavenly Father. We see the height of this in the crucifixion of Christ, where wisdom Himself is crucified, but where the power of God is also revealed. We understand the limits of earthly wisdom, for wisdom is not an impenetrable fortress that protects us from sin and folly. Also, wisdom is not a portable commodity. If Christ is true and ultimate wisdom, then the only way we can be wise is by seeking Christ. As John 15:5 says, "I am the vine, ye are the branches: he that abideth in me, and I in him, the same bringeth forth much fruit: for without me ye can do nothing." The only safe shelter we have in life from sin, indeed from ourselves, is in Christ.

If we wander from Christ, even the most inconsequential act of sin can be a fly in the ointment. I doubt that Adam and Eve fully grasped the devastating effect of eating a piece of fruit, not only on themselves but on the entire creation. Only Christ through the Spirit guides us to fear the Lord. Thus we must cling fast to every word of Christ and not veer to the left or the right. The Preacher says we must pursue wisdom at all costs. It is no matter if the wise are seemingly swept away like the wicked. No matter if the world uses our wisdom and then forgets to give us the praise. No matter if the world hates us for our wisdom in the face of its own folly or spurns the wisdom of God in Christ as foolishness. Indeed, the pursuit of wisdom at all costs is the message of the Preacher and of Christ, who says: "Again the kingdom of heaven is like unto treasure hid in a field; the which when a man hath found, he hideth, and for joy thereof goeth and selleth all that he hath, and buyeth that field. Again, the kingdom of heaven is like unto a merchant man, seeking goodly pearls: who, when he had found one pearl of great price, went and sold all that he had, and bought it" (Matt. 13:44–46).

Conclusion

The Preacher tells us to pursue wisdom at all costs because it is not a thing but a person, Jesus Christ. Pray that Christ by the Holy Spirit will fuel the passion in our hearts to desire Christ in all things and to have the mind of Christ, which is wisdom. Pray that we will continually cling to Him so that we will not see things as the world sees them but rather as Christ sees them. For in our weakness and humility, God manifests the glory of Christ.

STUDY QUESTIONS

1. In what ways have you observed the unpredictability of life? What has that taught
   you? Work, illness, sudden death of
   my brother, job loss etc. That the Lord is
2. In what ways does wisdom often go un-   Truly
   noticed and unrewarded? Why do you   in
   think that is? In the work place, because contro
   of personalities, favortism, politics
3. In what ways have you seen the limitations of wisdom? What did that teach
   you? Sometimes pride in all it's sin
   and ugliness, rears it's head. Lend on Christ
   and His Wisdom, not my own, because it's not
4. How does God manifest His wisdom   mine
   through the weak and foolish things of   nor is
   the world? Because in our weakness   it me.
   He shines through. He often uses   but it
   the simple things in life to reveal   Him.
   His wisdom. He takes what the
   world deems as weak, or foolish
   and uses that to confound their
   ideas

13
Cast Your Bread
on Waters

Read Ecclesiastes 10:8–11:6

We have learned that we must pursue wisdom at all costs. But the Preacher says life can be unpredictable, for the swift do not always win a race and the strong do not always win a battle. What is more, wisdom often goes unrecognized and unrewarded. However, the Preacher urges us to continue pursuing wisdom, which, in the light of the New Testament, is ultimately Christ, for God has made His Son our wisdom, righteousness, and sanctification, and in Christ are hidden the treasures of wisdom and knowledge.

The Preacher now continues his comparison of wisdom and folly, this time addressing the question whether we should simply surrender to the apparent unfairness of life. His answer is, "Not at all!" The Preacher will always commend wisdom over folly.

A Life of Wisdom

The Preacher begins by observing that sometimes we lose incentive to work, for we often encounter problems and obstacles. He says, "He that diggeth a pit shall fall into it; and whoso breaketh an hedge, a serpent shall bite him. Whoso removeth stones shall be hurt therewith; and he that cleaveth wood shall be endangered thereby" (Eccl. 10:8–9). Some of these observations seem simple to understand, while others require further explanation. If you dig a pit, chances are you will fall into it, the Preacher says. If you quarry stones, one may fall on you and injure you. If you split logs, your ax head may fly off its handle and injure or kill a co-worker. In the Preacher's day, homes were built of stones mortared together by mud. Sometimes the mud would dry out and leave crevices between the blocks, which were perfect places for serpents to hide. So if you were repairing your home, you might dig out the wall only to be bitten by a serpent.

With such grim warnings, we might think the best course of action is no action at all. Yet this is not what the Preacher advises. Rather, he once again contrasts both wisdom and folly to show the difference between the two. In verse 10, he says: "If the iron be blunt, and he doth not whet the edge, then must he put to more strength: but wisdom is profitable to direct." The Preacher is saying that if one pursues wisdom, it will help him work more effectively. The wise man is like a snake charmer who charms the snake before handling it (v. 11). The same cannot be said for the fool. Furthermore, the Preacher says, the words of a wise man win him favor, while a fool blathers on and on, and what he says eventually brings him misery (vv. 12–13). The Preacher amplifies this point in verses 14–15: "A fool also is full of words: a man cannot tell what shall be; and what shall be after him, who can tell him? The labour of the foolish wearieth every one of them, because he knoweth not how to go to the city."

Like a dog that chases his tail, the fool verbally runs around in circles and in the end accomplishes nothing. The Preacher illustrates the contrast between wisdom and folly with an example of foolish and wise kings. He says, "Woe to thee, O land, when thy king is a child, and thy princes eat in the morning! Blessed art thou, O land, when thy king is the son of nobles, and thy princes eat in due season, for strength, and not for drunkenness" (Eccl. 10:16–17)! What this means is that people whose king is young will be in trouble, for an immature ruler will not rule wisely. A wise ruler knows the proper time for a feast, while a childish one does not. This statement seems to reflect what eventually occurred with Israel's own rulers (Isa. 3:4–5; 5:11). The bottom line is that we should be diligent in labor, for that is wise, while sloughing off is foolish.

The Preacher continues to press this point, saying, "By much slothfulness the building decayeth; and through idleness of the hands the house droppeth through" (Eccl. 10:18). The fool looks at the potential dangers and pitfalls of life and ceases to work, saying, "What's the point?" But time and sloth is like gasoline and fire. If a fool fails to repair his roof, over time that inactivity will fuel a catastrophe. The roof will start to leak, and eventually the house will be destroyed. We might add another illustration here: if we fail to exercise and eat properly, we will over time become overweight, in poor health, and in danger of dying.

The Preacher also critiques the notion that we should labor just so we can eat and drink and be merry, for, of all God's gifts, money is the answer for everything (v. 19). The Preacher is not saying that money solves all problems, nor that we should turn money into an idol. However, of all of God's gifts, wealth can be the most useful. In this particular context, the Preacher is saying that one's labor yields wealth, or financial compensation, which has great benefit. So, the wise man does not give up on life but instead labors for pay. What is more, the wise man is not foolish, nor does he say foolish things, for some things are better left unsaid (v. 20).

The Preacher goes on to say, "Cast thy bread upon the waters: for thou shalt find it after many days. Give a portion to seven, and also to eight; for thou knowest not what evil shall be upon the earth" (Eccl. 11:1–2). If Ecclesiastes 10:20 says that the wise man exercises caution in all he does, verses 1–2 of chapter 11 tell us that he is not so timid that he refuses to take risks. He is willing to take some calculated risks, but he does not place all of his eggs in one basket. He is willing to take a chance and cast his bread upon the waters to see what happens. But he also spreads his interests between seven, if not eight, different investments so that if disaster strikes one or more, others may still be productive.

One way to understand what the Preacher says here is to compare these statements to what Proverbs says about the godly woman. The woman in Proverbs 31 is trusted by her husband; she works with her hands, works diligently, rises early in the morning, is a shrewd business woman, gives her husband a good reputation, and is filled with wisdom. Note that what is said of the godly woman may also be said of the godly wise man whom the Preacher describes. This thought is developed in verses 3–4 where the Preacher observes that the clouds move according to their own schedule, and trees fall without consulting anyone.

Yet verse 4 goes on to say: "He that observeth the wind shall not sow; and he that regardeth the clouds shall not reap." If a person waits for the perfect opportunity, he may never act because life is seldom if ever predictable. The one who forever watches the wind, waiting for the perfect opportunity, may never plant, and the one who waits for the clouds to drop rain might never reap. Perhaps the modern equivalent to verse 4 is, "He who hesitates is lost."

The wise man exhibits great confidence here, but it is not arrogance, for the Preacher says in the close of the section: "As thou knowest not what is the way of the spirit, nor how the bones do grow in the womb of her that is with child: even so thou knowest not the works of God who maketh all" (Eccl. 11:5). In the end, the Preacher bows before the mystery of God's all-wise providence. He does not pretend to know all the answers, nor does he pretend to know what will happen in the future. Nevertheless, he knows that he has been called to fear the Lord, and one way to do that is to use the good gifts that God has given him. That does not mean that he becomes dependent upon these gifts or turns them into idols, but rather that he seeks to be a faithful steward of the blessings that God has showered upon him. So the Preacher says, "In the morning sow thy seed, and in the evening withhold not thine hand: for thou knowest not whether shall prosper, either this or that, or whether they both shall be alike good" (Eccl. 11:6).

Seeking the Mind of Christ

As we reflect upon this passage from the vantage point of the New Testament and the revelation of Christ, we must remember that the Preacher has been commending wisdom and saying that the wise are not idle. From the Preacher's perspective, the wise man fears the Lord. From the past several chapters, we know that the pinnacle of the fear of the Lord is looking to Christ by faith. As we saw in the previous chapter and the beginning of this one, God has made Christ our wisdom. In Him all treasures of wisdom and knowledge are hidden.

In light of what God has done for us in Christ and by faith through the indwelling power and presence of the Holy Spirit, Christians should be marked by the wisdom of Christ. Because of our union with Christ, we should shine forth in righteousness and holiness. However, many in the church over the years have mistaken holiness and piety for seclusion from the world. This withdrawal is not simply physical, like a monk or nun staying within the confines of a monastery. This mindset can also affect Christians in the midst of the world. The saying "He's so heavenly minded that he's no earthly good" would trouble the Preacher, for a person with the mind of Christ is not so withdrawn that he is no earthly good. Rather, like the Preacher's wise man, he is willing to take calculated risks and is not fearful of the challenges or even setbacks of life. In the challenges and failures of life, he does not give way to folly, lethargy, or apathy. Instead, the wise person confidently makes diligent use of the good gifts that God has given him: his intellect, his decision-making ability, his knowledge, and his physical abilities, which are all governed by wisdom, or the mind of Christ.

The wise person is confident, not because of arrogance, but because of his confidence in what God his heavenly Father has done in Christ. As Romans 8:31–34 says,

> What shall we then say to these things? If God be for us, who can be against us? He that spared not his own Son, but delivered him up for us all, how shall he not with him also freely give us all things? Who shall lay any thing to the charge of God's elect? It is God that justifieth. Who is he that condemneth? It is Christ that died, yea rather, that is risen again, who is even at the right hand of God, who also maketh intercession for us.

One who is shaped by Christ is confident, not in himself, but in Christ. One whose mind is molded by Christ through the Holy Spirit is diligent in all he does, not for his own glory, advancement, or wealth. Rather, he seeks in all things to bring glory to his heavenly Father, to Christ, and to the Holy Spirit. When praised by his fellow man, he does not take the credit but acknowledges that the Triune Lord deserves the glory. As Paul says to the

Corinthians, in whatever we do, whether we eat or drink, we should do all things to the glory of God (1 Cor. 10:31).

One indwelt by Christ also labors diligently to serve his fellow man. So often we look upon unbelievers as inferior because they do not acknowledge Christ as Lord. We think that therefore Christians are superior. Yet such a mindset is contrary to the mind of Christ. Christ did not look upon unbelievers as inferior but with mercy. He came to serve those who despised Him. What Christ did in His earthly ministry, He continues through the church in the world today. In this regard, we must not build castles in the sand to make our name great but instead be diligent in all of our labors to serve our fellow man and to extend to them the kindness and grace of God in Christ.

Conclusion

Let it never be said of us that we are foolish and slothful because we have given up on life. We who are being renewed in the image of Christ through the Holy Spirit are to shine forth the righteousness and holiness of our God. We are called to manifest the wisdom of Christ in everything that we do.

STUDY QUESTIONS

1. In a seemingly futile existence, when are we most tempted to quit trying? What does the Preacher say about that? *During trials, hard times. Pursue wisdom, stay confident in God*

2. What is the difference between confidence and arrogance in doing the works of God? *Confidence leans on God, knows that it is God who is enabling him, not himself*

3. In whom does the Christian find his confidence? Explain how that works. *God/Christ. By learning of Christ, growing in Him.*

4. In what ways should the church diligently labor with confidence? *In the midst of secularism and persecution, stay the course, cling to Christ, trust in His completed work for us.*

14
Remember Your Creator

Read Ecclesiastes 11:7–12:8

The Preacher has contrasted wisdom and folly as it pertains to living life. He showed how the randomness of life would shake a fool into timidity and sloth. In fear of the apparent dangers of life, the fool retreats to the safety of inactivity. But the wise man who trusts in the Lord has confidence in the providence of God. He does not fear life, even in the uncertainties of life, but goes forward with boldness and industriousness. Through the life, death, resurrection, and ascension of Christ, we understand the Preacher's point more clearly. Knowing what God has done for us in Christ, we may entrust ourselves to the care of our heavenly Father, knowing that if Christ is for us, no one can destroy that confidence. That encourages us to be bold, not for ourselves, but for the sake of Christ.

It also encourages us to be industrious, not so we can build worldly enterprises to make our name great, but to bring glory to our heavenly Father.

Now the Preacher describes two great seasons in one's life: youth and old age. To summarize this passage, we might say, "We're not always sixteen and bullet-proof. So go ahead and enjoy your youth, but do so mindful of your end and of your Creator." We will go on to note several images the Preacher includes in this passage, but also how these observations ultimately point us to Christ and our need for Him. For apart from Christ, we live a vain and futile existence.

A Sober Assessment

The passage begins with a sober assessment of life: "Truly the light is sweet, and a pleasant thing it is for the eyes to behold the sun: but if a man live many years, and rejoice in them all; yet let him remember the days of darkness; for they shall be many. All that cometh is vanity" (Eccl. 11:7–8). The Preacher says we may experience many good and joyous days in life, but we will also have dark days. The longer we live, the more we will see of sadness, trial, illness, or death. These dark times do not take away the pleasant and joyful times in one's life, however, but may add to their sweetness.

Light may not be fully appreciated on a bright and sunny day, whereas in the pitch black of night we prize the light that pierces the darkness and illumines our way. The Preacher therefore tells his readers to enjoy their youth:

> Rejoice, O young man, in thy youth; and let thy heart cheer thee in the days of thy youth, and walk in the ways of thine heart, and in the sight of thine eyes: but know thou, that for all these things God will bring thee into judgment. Therefore remove sorrow from thy heart, and put away evil from thy flesh: for childhood and youth are vanity (Eccl. 11:9–10).

The Preacher encourages his readers to enjoy the blessings and joys of youth, especially in the face of the dark days that all people will experience as they age.

The Preacher does not encourage profligate living, however, in which a young man casts wisdom aside to seek debauchery on one drunken bender after another. He reminds us that God watches all that we do and that He will one day bring us to judgment. The Preacher thus counsels the young, saying, "Remember now thy Creator in the days of thy youth, while the evil days come not, nor the years draw nigh, when thou shalt say, I have no pleasure in them" (Eccl. 12:1). The Preacher reminds the young to remember their Creator. This reminds us that ultimately we will find no satisfaction in life apart from a right relationship with our Creator. Sure, we may have moments of joy and happiness, but we will also experience times of sadness and darkness in which we can only find solace in Christ.

Some people desperately cling to youth to prolong the good times, sometimes at great cost. But this pursuit of happiness ends in sadness because man discovers that he finds no satisfaction in pleasures that are fleeting. The Preacher's statements here are evocative of Solomon, who pursued every pleasure in life but in the end found no satisfaction in them. He died surrounded by wealth and wives, and his kingdom was torn apart and given to two of his sons. The words of a contemporary song express the never-ending quest for satisfaction and rest: "All my life I've been searching for something, Something never comes, never leads to nothing, Nothing satisfies, but I'm getting close, Closer to the prize at the end of the rope."

The Preacher goes on to provide various images of young men who eventually become old and die. He says in verse 2 that the sun and the moon eventually go dark. In verse 3 he says that the keeper of the house, who was strong, eventually grows old and begins to tremble. The man who stood tall and strong eventually becomes bent and gnarled with age. In verse 4 the Preacher contrasts the noise and activity that young people hear during the day with the low rumble that old people, who are hard of hearing, can only hear. In youth, we might be awakened by the sound of singing birds and the songs of young children playing in the street, but when we grow old, the doors to our houses are shut and we no longer hear the sound of people in the streets. When we are young, we stride through the city unafraid of anything, but as we grow old we become fearful of "what is high" and "in the way" (v. 5).

In the latter part of verse 5, the Preacher talks about a blossoming almond tree. That becomes significant when we realize that the blossoms are white. So the Preacher says that when the young man grows old, his hair begins to gray, then white. He also describes the grasshopper, which usually hops along at great distances, but drags itself along the ground as it ages. The Preacher offers a series of images to show that life, for the young, is fragile enough, but weakness is magnified in old age.

In verse 6 the Preacher writes of a silver cord that is snapped and a golden bowl that is broken. He is likely describing a lamp that hangs from a chain, but when the chain breaks, the lamp falls and breaks what is under it, such as an earthen bowl used to serve food and water. Likewise, the end of verse 6 speaks of a water pitcher that is shattered at the fountain, perhaps because its handle breaks off or the pitcher simply gives way to long-term use. These images occupy the Preacher's mind because, as he writes at the end of verse 5, man is going to his eternal home as mourners walk about the streets. In verse 7 he says, "Then shall the dust return to the earth as it was: and the spirit shall return unto God who gave it."

Once again we see the fragility of life. Despite all of his accomplishments, his intellect, his aesthetic qualities, and his monuments, in the end man ages, dies, and returns to dust. This makes the Preacher repeat the refrain that appears so often in his book: "Vanity of vanities, saith the preacher; all is vanity" (Eccl. 12:8). The Preacher is not saying that all of life is vanity. What is vanity is the young man who fails to remember his Creator. What he does is futile and vain because he thinks that he has the world by the tail but then ends up as an old man who is led around by the world which tells him where to go, buries him, then lets him dissolve in dust.

Remembering Christ in Our Youth

We should note three important things here. First, remember that the Preacher tells us to remember our Creator in the days of our youth (Eccl. 12:1). Second, he says that as man gets old and dies, he goes to his eternal home (Eccl. 12:5). Third, he says "God will bring thee into judgment" for all our actions (Eccl. 11:9). We see this theme repeated by Christ, who says: "But I say unto you, that every idle word that men shall speak, they shall give account thereof in the day of judgment. For by thy words thou shalt be justified, and by thy words thou shalt be condemned" (Matt. 12:36–37).

So then, three things indicate the foolish young man is on a path of disaster. He lives his life in futility as his strength withers away under the scorching heat of time, then he dies, and then he goes to his eternal home. Before going to that home, however, he meets his Creator. And that Creator judges him, then sends him to his eternal home, which is eternal death, or hell. So the Preacher says, even in our youth we must remember our Creator, who the New Testament tells us is Christ (John 1:1–3; Col. 1:15–16). In light of the revelation of Christ, the Preacher tells all of us, but especially the young, to remember Christ.

To remember Christ is not to think of Him once in a while but rather to believe in Him. It is trusting in His life of perfect obedience lived in our place; His perfect sacrifice suffered on our behalf; His resurrection, which conquered sin and death; and His ascension, after which He was placed at the right hand of the Father. This frees us from the fear of judgment for our sin and gives us hope in facing death. The young person who fails to remember Christ and goes about his life as if He did not exist not only wastes his life in the foolish pursuit of contentment but also renders himself liable to the judgment of Christ on the Last Day.

But for those who look to Christ, there is hope as well as purpose. Paul tells the Corinthians that even when we face death, with our outward man wasting away, our inward man is renewed. He tells the Corinthians to look beyond the things that are transient to those things that are eternal. He offers a message of hope in characterizing our present existence as dwelling in a bodily tent that will one day give way to a heavenly dwelling of resurrection bodies (2 Cor. 4:16–5:5). Paul knows that old age comes even to the believer, but in life the believer does not pursue the foolishness of looking for satisfaction in temporal fleeting things but finds his hope in Christ.

Christ offers us contentment in the present by giving us the Holy Spirit. The Holy Spirit comforts us, assures of Christ's love for us even in the most dire circumstances, and gives us the hope of eternal life. So we look forward to the shedding of our earthly body and being clothed in our glorious resurrection body. Note the contrast between the Preacher's characterization of the foolish young man who grows old and dies, then returns to the dust. But of the one who looks to Christ by faith and forgets not his Creator in the days of his youth, Paul says: "The first man is of the earth, earthy: the second man is the Lord from heaven. As is the earthy, such are they also that are earthy: and as is the heavenly, such are they also that are heavenly. And as we have borne the image of the earthy, we shall also bear the image of the heavenly" (1 Cor. 15:47–49).

We therefore live today in the presence of Christ through the work of the Holy Spirit, who gives us hope for eternal life. Through Christ, we live with hope and direct our lives towards the goal of glorifying Christ and building His kingdom. Throughout our lives, but especially in our youth, we must expend all our energy, labors, intellect, and hopes in remembering our Creator, who is Christ.

Conclusion

Young people and old, and everyone between, must not squander life in the idolatrous pursuit of their own desires but instead pursue the things of Christ. Do our pursuits honor Christ, or do they reflect the foolish pursuit of things that in the end will never satisfy but bring us to dust and eternal death?

STUDY QUESTIONS

1. How do most young people today live their lives? What are their goals, their dreams? How do they spend most of their time and energy? For what? *Live for today as if they will never grow old, without much caution.*

2. What eventually happens to all young people? *They grow old, views change, then death. Become/never satisified*

3. How does the Preacher tell young people to live their lives? *With their Creator in mind.*

4. When the Preacher tells us to remember our Creator, who does he ultimately have in mind? *Jesus Christ / God*

5. What does it mean to *remember* Christ? How do you do that in your life? *Always have Him before you, thinking of Him, learning about and from Him, desiring Him*

15
Our One Shepherd

Read Ecclesiastes 12:9–14

The Preacher has advised people not to forget their Creator when they are young. In the Preacher's day, as in our own, young people thought they were bullet-proof and could therefore pursue vain desires to find satisfaction. The Preacher reminded us that young people become old and ultimately unhappy because they have not sought contentment in their covenant Lord. Hence, the Preacher says we must remember the Creator in the days of our youth. In the revelation of Christ, the Preacher's ultimate call is that we are mindful of Christ all of the days of our life.

We now come to the end of Ecclesiastes, where we find some closing words of wisdom, which apparently were not written by the Preacher but by an editor. Still, these words are as divinely

inspired as those of the Preacher. The identity of
the editor, like that of the author of the book,
is unknown. However, that does not lessen the
impact of his counsel. The conclusion of the book
can be divided into three parts: the preacher (vv.
9–10), the purpose of wisdom (vv. 11–12), and
final words of wisdom (vv. 13–14).

1. *The Preacher* (vv. 9–10)

Ecclesiastes concludes with a description of the
Preacher. He was most certainly a wise man, for
this is evident in the previous twelve chapters of
Ecclesiastes. However, he was also a person who
observed, studied, and explored many things and
wrote many proverbs. In many ways this description is true of King Solomon, to whom the Lord
poured out His wisdom (1 Kings 4:29–34). Yet in
many respects, it is quite easy for us to misunder-
stand the nature of Solomon and the Preacher's
quest for wisdom. The Preacher studied and taught
knowledge, while Solomon spoke of beasts, birds,
reptiles, and fish. It seems that both Solomon and
the Preacher were interested in the pursuit of scientific knowledge. But that fails to account for
their overall pursuit of wisdom. Wisdom is not
knowledge, though the two overlap, but rather
wisdom is applied knowledge. More specifically,
the Bible defines wisdom as the beginning of
knowledge and the fear of the Lord. The fool says

in his heart there is no God, Scripture tells us. So if scientific knowledge is not the goal, why would the Preacher and Solomon pursue knowledge, even in the study of nature?

The answer may be in Paul's statement from Romans 1:20: "For the invisible things of him from the creation of the world are clearly seen, being understood by the things that are made, even his eternal power and Godhead; so that they are without excuse." Here Paul tells us, in effect, that God has written two books: Scripture and the book of nature. Scripture tells us about the gospel of Christ, which is not published in the book of nature. However, when we read nature through the lens of Scripture, we can read it rightly, not simply absorbing scientific knowledge but following God's footsteps so that we think God's thoughts after Him. In this way we learn wisdom.

Solomon thus could observe nature and learn about God's wisdom, writing such proverbs as: "Go to the ant, thou sluggard; consider her ways, and be wise" (Prov. 6:6). Likewise, the Preacher described the aging grasshopper that dragged itself along the ground (Eccl. 12:5) to show that all things must come to an end. In the Preacher's study of knowledge or in Solomon's study of nature, each sought to write "words of truth" (v. 10). In this regard we should ask ourselves how we view the world. Do we recognize that Christ has created everything that was made, and that

nothing that has been made was made apart from
Him? Do we realize that Christ created everything,
visible and invisible, including thrones, principalities, and dominions?

By using the lens of Scripture, we can read
the book of nature and learn the wisdom of
our mighty Lord and Savior. We can behold the
mighty surf as it pounds upon the shore. We can
gaze into the eye of a storm with its flashes of
lightning and rumblings of thunder and glimpse
at the power of our Creator. We can know that
Christ, with a single word, can bring such forces
of nature into submission, as He once did in calm-
ing the storm on the Sea of Galilee. We can look
at the intricacy of creation in the industriousness
of the ant or the complexity of DNA, or see the
simple but deadly power of a germ, thereby seeing a reflection of the complexity of God. We then
ask ourselves: who can plumb the depths of God's
mind or be His counselor? We see the complexity
of God's providence in providing us with the way
of salvation, but also the simplicity of preaching
the gospel. We may then glory in the wisdom of
God in Christ, as Paul writes: "Because the foolishness of God is wiser than men; and the weakness
of God is stronger than men" (1 Cor. 1:25).

2. *The Purpose of Wisdom* (vv. 11–12)
As we contemplate Christ's wisdom in creation,

we should also keep the purpose of wisdom in mind. The editor tells us:

> The words of the wise are as goads, and as nails fastened by the masters of assemblies, which are given from one shepherd. And further, by these, my son, be admonished: of making many books there is no end; and much study is a weariness of the flesh (Eccl. 12:11–12).

Some people think of wisdom as a series of rules. Perhaps that is because many want to be told what to do rather than to seek after wisdom. A legalist loves the law because he believes obedience to it will save him and guide him in every circumstance of life. The editor in Ecclesiastes refutes this. He says wisdom is nothing more than a goad or a nail firmly fixed to a wall. Wisdom offers observations or principles that are in no way exhaustive. So the editor warns us against looking for anything more. If we looked for a rule for every single circumstance in life, we would need an infinite rulebook. So the editor says, "Of making many books there is no end; and much study is a weariness of the flesh" (v. 12). Think, for example, of King Solomon's ruling about two women who each claimed to be mother of the same child. There were no rulebooks for such a dilemma; it required the application of wisdom. So we read of Solomon's decision: "And all Israel heard of the judgment which the king had judged;

and they feared the king: for they saw that the wisdom of God was in him, to do judgment" (1 Kings 3:28).

What is particularly amazing about Solomon's decision is that it demonstrated wisdom from the king rather than from the use of the *urim* and *thumim*, which was one of God's way of revealing His will on difficult decisions. Here the king applied wisdom to the situation and proclaimed a just judgment. As we have seen in the rest of Ecclesiastes, Solomon foreshadows Christ, who is wisdom incarnate (Col. 2:3).

This might make us uneasy, for we know we must not lean on our own understanding, yet the law of God does not tell us what to do in every situation. So we are left with question marks in certain areas of life. Yes, the law is definitive in moral issues, so there is no justification for murder, adultery, thievery, coveting, and the like. However, it is not so definitive about other things in life, such as confronting a fool. Solomon offers us the seemingly contradictory advice: "Answer not a fool according to his folly, lest thou also be like unto him. Answer a fool according to his folly, lest he be wise in his own conceit" (Prov. 26:4–5). So, when do you answer and when do you stay silent? The decision calls for wisdom, Solomon says, which can only be found in God.

Remember, the Shepherd gives wisdom. As we have seen throughout Ecclesiastes, that Shepherd is Christ, in whom are hidden all the treasures of wisdom and knowledge. We must therefore seek the mind of Christ, as Paul tells the Philippians, or, as he tells the Romans, seek to have our minds transformed by Christ through the power of the Spirit by the application of the Word to our hearts. All of life, whether at home, in marriage, in raising children, dealing with family, or interacting with people at work, calls for wisdom. Only Christ through the Spirit can equip us for such situations so that we will know how to apply the knowledge of God in answering or not answering the words of a fool.

3. *Final Words of Wisdom* (vv. 13–14)
In the final verses of chapter 12, the editor sums up the Book of Ecclesiastes as well as the pursuit of wisdom: "Let us hear the conclusion of the whole matter: Fear God, and keep his commandments: for this is the whole duty of man. For God shall bring every work into judgment, with every secret thing, whether it be good, or whether it be evil" (Eccl. 12:13–14). The ultimate goal of the wise person is to fear the Lord and keep His commandments. The wise person sees himself as one of God's creatures rather than his own creator. But he also recognizes his sinfulness and knows that he will have to account for all of his words, thoughts, and deeds.

So the wise man seeks shelter in God and in

His wisdom, which is revealed in Christ (1 Cor. 1:18–24). The cross of Christ reveals the wisdom of God only to those whom God has given eyes to see, ears to hear, and faith to trust in Jesus and His cross-centered wisdom. The mark of wisdom is to know who God is, what He demands of us in holiness, the exactitude of the Law, and our inability to reach this mark. Wisdom seeks shelter in the One who alone has met the mark and who has suffered on behalf of those who look to Him by faith. With the eyes of God-given faith, we may see things, not as the world sees them, but according to the wisdom of God.

Conclusion

In God's wisdom revealed in Christ, we see not only our need for Christ but also the meaning of our existence. We thus seek the mind of Christ in all things, recognizing the limits of the Law, which can only condemn our sin, not deliver us from it. We seek the mind of Christ so that He will manifest Himself in us and that we might, by the power of the Spirit, be obedient to God. We then apply this wisdom to every area of life as we behold the great glory and might of our faithful covenant Lord.

STUDY QUESTIONS

1. What two books has God written?

2. How does wisdom function? Does wisdom give specific rules for every circumstance in life? Describe some situations that are *applied* not directly addressed by Scripture. *Wisdom is* ^ *Knowledge, no, wisdom seeks the mind of Christ*

3. How does Solomon foreshadow Christ as it pertains to wisdom? *He was the wisest man, sought wisdom from God.*

4. What will the wise person ultimately do? *Seek wisdom and shelter in Christ*

Christ is that wisdom

→ *Prayer and searching the Scriptures ~~will be~~ the way to IS Seek guidance in those types of situation, lean on Christ*

Conclusion

Now that you have read this book, I hope you have a better understanding of Ecclesiastes, which finds its fulfillment in the crucified and resurrected Messiah. Like Solomon, our prayer should be that God in Christ through the Spirit will transform our minds according to the mind of Christ. With the mind of Christ, the ambiguities of life are less troublesome because we realize that, even in the midst of darkness and shadows, we do not lean upon our own understanding but seek shelter beneath the wings of Christ. We realize that God uses every event in life, whether joy or sorrow, as a crucible in which to purge sin out of us and make us holy. Through Ecclesiastes we can rejoice as we reflect upon life under the sun, knowing there is more to our existence than vanity and futility because Christ has redeemed us and given us eternal life. *Soli Deo gloria!*

The Rule of Love:
Broken, Fulfilled, and Applied

J. V. Fesko

Hardcover, 152 pages   ISBN 978-1-60178-063-8

"*The Rule of Love* refreshingly sets each of the Ten Commandments in its historical, covenantal, and redemptive context, then proceeds to show that each commandment covers a broad range of issues that convict us as believers of sin and encourage us to flee to Christ who is the great Law-fulfiller and our complete remedy for all our Law-breaking. Dr. Fesko masterfully sets each commandment in the light of Christ and shows how each is connected to the church and to every believer today. In this book, which is the most Christ-centered treatment of the Law I have ever read, biblical, systematic, and practical theology wonderfully coalesce in a harmonious whole."

—Dr. Joel R. Beeke, President of
Puritan Reformed Theological Seminary,
Grand Rapids, Michigan

The Seven Signs:

Seeing the Glory of Christ in the Gospel of John

Anthony T. Selvaggio

Paperback, 128 pages
ISBN 978-1-60178-083-6

A major component of Jesus' ministry on earth was the performance of signs and wonders. In this book, Anthony T. Selvaggio uses the seven signs given in the first half of the Gospel of John to navigate us toward a glorious destination. This journey begins at a wedding and ends at a funeral. Throughout this trip you will witness the incredible events of water being turned into wine, the temple cleansed, a sick boy restored, a lame man brought to his feet, thousands fed, a blind man gaining sight, and a dead man coming forth from his tomb. While this tour centers in the land of Palestine, it will ultimately take you beyond the finiteness of this created world. For on this majestic journey, you will see more than mere signs and wonders—you will see the glory of Jesus the Christ, the Son of God!

"Jesus' messianic signs are at the very heart of John's theological message. *The Seven Signs* is delightfully written, theologically sound, and spiritually nurturing. I highly recommend it!"

—Andreas J. Köstenberger, Director of Ph.D. Studies and Professor of New Testament at Southeastern Baptist Theological Seminary in Wake Forest, North Carolina

Contagious Christian Living

Joel R. Beeke

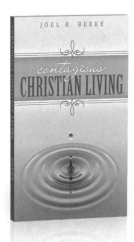

Paperback, 144 pages
ISBN 978-1-60178-079-9

When some people smile, they ignite smiles in people around them. They have contagious smiles. If that's what a contagious smile is, what is contagious Christian living? It is living that is so godly and so consistent that people around them cannot help but be impacted and inspired. In *Contagious Christian Living*, Joel R. Beeke looks at four people in the Bible to find out how people today can live an influential life in dependence on the Holy Spirit. Here is your invitation to read about, and pray for, the sacrificial submission of Jephthah's daughter, the Christ-centeredness of Bartimaeus, the contagious blessings of Jacob, and the consistent integrity of Daniel.

"One of Joel Beeke's best books yet. Absorb it yourself and buy copies for your church. Anyone who wants to grow spiritually will benefit enormously and eternally from these sermons."

—Edward Donnelly, Minister at
Trinity Reformed Presbyterian Church,
Newtownabbey, Northern Ireland